D1570828

MIRACLE OF
THE MUSIC MAN

MIRACLE OF
THE MUSIC MAN

THE CLASSIC AMERICAN STORY
OF MEREDITH WILLSON

MARK CABANISS

FOREWORD BY RUPERT HOLMES

ROWMAN & LITTLEFIELD
Lanham • Boulder • New York • London

Published by Rowman & Littlefield
An imprint of The Rowman & Littlefield Publishing Group, Inc.
4501 Forbes Blvd., Ste. 200
Lanham, MD 20706
www.rowman.com

86-90 Paul Street, London EC2A 4NE

British Library Cataloguing in Publication Information available

Library of Congress Cataloging-in-Publication Data

Names: Cabaniss, Mark, author.
Title: Miracle of The Music Man : the classic American story of Meredith Willson / Mark Cabaniss.
Description: Lanham : Rowman & Littlefield, [2022]. | Includes index. | Summary: "Mark Cabaniss brings to life the rocky origins of this timeless show, the music behind it, and the against-all-odds success story of its creator. Interweaving behind-the-scenes perspectives, this book looks at Meredith Willson's unusual career as a composer, conductor, radio personality, and flutist, which reached its pinnacle in The Music Man"—Provided by publisher.
Identifiers: LCCN 2022014910 (print) | LCCN 2022014911 (ebook) | ISBN 9781538154649 (cloth) | ISBN 9781538154656 (epub)
Subjects: LCSH: Willson, Meredith, 1902–1984. | Willson, Meredith, 1902–1984. Music man. | Composers—United States—Biography.
Classification: LCC ML410.W714 C33 2022 (print) | LCC ML410.W714 (ebook)
| DDC 780.92 [B]—dc23/eng/20220520
LC record available at https://lccn.loc.gov/2022014910
LC ebook record available at https://lccn.loc.gov/2022014911

To Meredith Willson . . . and all people who truly "see the band" and believe in the transforming power of music.

CONTENTS

ACKNOWLEDGMENTS

I wish to first thank Michael Tan, associate acquisitions editor at Rowman & Littlefield, for believing in this book and his expert editorial input throughout my writing process. Michael was ever patient with my schedule and consistently offered me encouraging words while skillfully and kindly keeping me on the right track. Thanks, Michael! Also, thanks to the entire, incredible team at Rowman & Littlefield for helping bring this book to life.

Next, to the late Rosemary Willson, my deep thanks for her kindness to me in opening her home and heart on several occasions with the stories and thoughts she personally shared with me regarding Meredith. Her love of Meredith was palpable, and of all the things she said to me that resonated most was that "Meredith was as warm in private as he was in public."

Unending thanks goes to Tom Camp of Gang, Tyre, Raymer, Brown & Passman in Beverly Hills, California—the storied law firm who represented Meredith Willson then . . . and now. Tom's support and blessing of this book made it possible. Also, to Sarah Lyding, executive director of The Music Man Foundation for her support and interest in this project. Between Tom and Sarah, Meredith's legacy is forever safe, assured, and growing.

I am most grateful to Chris Lewis of Michael Feinstein's Great American Songbook Foundation (GASF). Chris happily gave me remarkable access to pictures, files, and personal papers of Meredith (expertly archived at the GASF, donated by Rosemary Willson), which add immensely to this book.

To Drew Cohen and the awesome team at Music Theatre International: Thank you for your support of this book and the amazing job you do to perpetuate The Music Man in specific and musical theatre in general.

Also, my heartfelt gratitude to Dotty Dickson. She believed in me when I was a mere twenty-one-year-old college student when she insisted to my hometown community theatre that I was capable of conducting a twenty-piece pit orchestra for our production of *The Music Man*, thus beginning my everlasting fascination with and inspiration from the show and its creator. Also to Frances Welch, Helen Krause, Brenda Crosby Bouser, Stan Hardin, and Suzy Welch Sheets for their roles in that wonderful experience.

For my dear friend Jane Kelley, who pulled me out of my self-imposed retirement from the stage to perform the role of Harold Hill under her direction in *The Music Man*: Thanks, Jane. That's now checked off my bucket list.

Finally, to my family plus Daniel Christian, Floyd and Aleeta Christian, and The Scheurens—my "Tennessee Family"—my love and thanks for your never-ending support in sharing and multiplying my joy.

With beautiful folks such as these in the world, I'll always believe there's a band.

FOREWORD

When I set out to explain the premise of my first musical at the invitation of its future Broadway producer—the legendary Joseph Papp of The New York Shakespeare Festival and The Public Theatre—he already knew my work as a songwriter and arranger for Barbra Streisand, my tunes covered by Barry Manilow, Dionne Warwick, Dolly Parton, and from my often-theatrical recordings of my own songs (which is how Joe knew me best). He asked me who was writing the musical's book (meaning the script itself, describing story, plot, characters, all action on stage and all spoken dialogue . . . in short, anything that isn't a musical number with or without lyrics). I told him, "Well, *I'm* writing the book as well as the music and lyrics. And of course, I always write my own orchestrations."

"Can you do that?" he asked, his eyes clearly searching my features for signs of incipient derangement. Joe had, after all, already brought many great Broadway stage musicals to life, including *A Chorus Line*, the revival of *Pirates of Penzance* and the earliest incarnation of *Hair*.

I put his mind at ease (*right*) with all the false bravado I could summon. "Well, I've been writing story songs for years now, with the constraint that they have to rhyme and can only be three minutes in length. To have two hours to tell a story without being obliged to rhyme every line, that's such a relief!"

In the back of my mind, I also held fast to my boyhood discovery that a fellow named Meredith Willson had managed to write music, lyrics, and book to one of the world's greatest Broadway musicals fairly much singlehandedly. (Yes, he did have Franklin Lacey as a coauthor and other talents handled the orchestrations, but as musicals go, I'd always known *The Music Man* was pretty much the output of a one-man band). I was very grateful to Mr. Willson at that particular moment because his stunning achievement may have given Joe Papp just enough reason to think I might be able to pull off such a coup despite this being my first musical, as had been the case with Meredith Willson.

The story of the creation and impact of that first milestone musical by Mr. Willson is the enthralling true-life tale that your author Mark Cabaniss is about to convey to you, and I view Mr. Cabaniss to be the single individual best suited and most qualified for this mission.

But first, as someone who has loved this miraculous musical and whose career was so deeply affected by it, I'd like to share with you how I first came to know and feel about *The Music Man*.

ß

When Walt Disney first developed plans for a new kind of amusement park, he decided that no matter which attraction (and its surrounding realm) most interested the paying guest—Jungle Cruise, Rocket to the Moon, mule train through the Painted Desert, or Peter Pan's flight to Neverland—one could only access these attractions' realms via the theme park's Main Street. As a boy, watching the opening day of the Magic Kingdom on the ABC network, not in Disney's "Wonderful World of Color" but 1955's Magnificent Monde of Monochrome, I wondered why anyone on the planet would want to spend time at a prosaic shooting gallery in Frontierland when they could be seduced into committing merry mayhem on Mr. Toad's Wild Ride . . . or for that matter, why would you want to spend time on a midwestern high street when you might very well have traveled from Des Moines solely to see what Disney hath wrought in Anaheim.

But whether you were eager to visit Disney's world of tomorrow, wild west, Afro-Polynesian jungle, or timeless fairy tale fiefdom, he devised it that all other realms could only be accessed by perambulating down a world cherished by Disney himself: a lyrical, idealized Midwest main street as it existed before the horseless carriage forever seized the reins of our lives. It was a town and time compatible with the background cels of *Lady and the Tramp* and—surprise—Disney's real home of Marceline, Missouri.

And if you were in Marceline and could hop aboard a regularly scheduled crow and fly it precisely north for a few hours, you would shortly arrive at Mason City, Iowa, home of one Meredith Willson, who would have been ten when the fictive Professor Harold Hill came plying his promises to local Iowans in 1912. Like Disney, Willson had a memory (and unblinking vision) of an Ice Cream Sociable world, frozen in time during an eternal summer: a faultlessly straightlaced midwestern town, one he wished to depict so winningly and wittily for us that no matter where else you might wander in musical theatre, savoring the phantoms of Paris, the cockneys of Covent Garden, the street gangs of New York's slums, or the denizens of the Eternal City (Emerald), at some point you would be happily required to sashay up the main street of River City, Iowa with seventy-six trombones hard on your heels.

I was ten myself when *The Music Man* premiered in the immediate wake of another instant Broadway classic, *My Fair Lady*. Although my father was a top Juilliard graduate, jazz musician and NBC staff conductor, my musical tastes were often steered by my British mother who loved the lyrics of Lorenz Hart and Noel Coward. For her, Lerner and Lowe's elegant high tea had it all over Willson's ebullient town picnic.

During this time frame, around my own home town of Nyack, New York (whose mansard-roofed Victorian gingerbreads lined the village's dreamy North and South Broadway, neatly bisected by a Main Street where my grandfather had once operated a dry goods store), these words were often heard among my crowd: "My parents got tickets to see the best musical on Broadway!" followed by a dramatic pause and the chip-on-shoulder challenge: "*Music Man!*" (By the way, everyone had dropped the *The* from its title two days after it opened.) One could define oneself by which of the two shows (*Lady* or *Man*) you (a) had seen, (b) hoped to see, (c) hoped they made into a movie first (for those of us who knew our families could never afford a Broadway show) or, more realistically, (d) had recently purchased at your local record store in the form of its original cast album. *My Fair Lady* was a Columbia record album with a serious black-and-gray label; no nonsense here. *Music Man* was Capitol, with its much-admired color wheel label. In the climate of those times, you were really expected to choose. One show had nothing but British accents, from refined to 'orrible; the other was sung in good ol' *Amurican*. One showcased dazzling wordplay and a scholar's vocabulary; the other was plain-spoken, so ordinary people could enjoy it.

Much as I wanted to earn my mother's approval, I found myself secretly enjoying *M.M.*'s fresh-from-the-oven theatrical apple pie served up with a satisfying slab of Wisconsin cheese. I mean, was there anyone on the planet who didn't love "76 Trombones" on first listen, the *Stars and Stripes Forever* for non-flag-wavers? (Willson's extended tour of duty with the Sousa band infiltrates every propulsive moment of the score.) I also had a comedy album where Stan Freberg opted to play it straight on one cut, and I found myself dropping the needle to secretly lip-sync to his rendition of "Trouble" over and over again; I was as swayed by the unrelenting sales pitch of its brilliant lyric as Professor Hill's conned townspeople were at the Majestic Theatre each night.

I admit I *was* troubled by how readily a number of the score's jauntier melodies were suitable fodder for the TV show *Sing Along with Mitch*, with their bilious "sound" of a lot of old white guys singing in unison to a bass, drum, rhythm guitar and accordion in cheap reverb. But then Rockland's All-County Junior High School Band (for which I was clarinet concertmaster) played *Selections from The Music Man*. To me, no Broadway musical ever took so readily to concert band instrumentation . . . because that sound was at the very soul of its score, of course.

I began to sense the sleight-of-hand of Willson's craft, for it was easy to process these songs as if they were older and more entrenched in the past than they really were. (Another telling indication of this phenomenon is that when you visit Main Street, United States, at Disneyland and get a lemonade in one of their sunny, turn-of-the-century pavilions, you'll often hear the score of *Music Man* being played over the speakers as if that music had existed in the evoked time frame whereas of course the musical debuted four years *after* Disneyland was unveiled!)

As a teenager, I believed that Willson's lyrics were bland as a vanilla milkshake. But with the passing years, I began to understand that they were artfully straightforward and deceptively subtle. Willson never wears his cleverness on his red-striped shirt sleeve, a self-effacing quality which allows the audience to believe the lyrics are being expressed by the characters for the very first time, employing the sometimes stiff or unromantic vocabulary that is native to their upbringing. Perhaps the most impressive moment in the lilting lyric of "Till There Was You" are three words that tiptoe by almost unnoticed (my boldface ahead): *And there was music and there were won-derful roses,* **they tell me,** *in sweet fragrant meadows of dawn and dew.* . . . The character of Marian asides, as a "thrown-away" passing thought, that she herself was so oblivious to the wonders of love that she had to be filled in by others as to what she'd been missing (and perhaps also that she was so swept away by these feelings that she could not take note of them as they finally had their way with her).

Of course, when the Beatles on their first American album decided to show they weren't all "vulgar noise" and possessed some musical sensitivity, they did so by singing "Till There Was You" with acoustic guitars (George's unplugged solo was particularly tasteful); I'm still trying to figure out why Paul sang "Never sawr them winging, no I never sawr them at all" . . . after all, he never sang "I Sawr Her Standing There." For many adults at the time, though, this was proof that the Beatles were listenable. For me, it was merely proof that *The Music Man* had a score that could be sung by Etta Johns, Ray Charles, Anita Bryant, Nana Mouskouri and Sergio Franco without anyone being injured in the process.

In terms of a unified theory of the American heartland, Willson's score and story were timeless on arrival; they were never stapled to a particular era except the hybrid landscape that existed in the heart and sensibilities of Mere-dith Willson's musical loves and personal experience.

On a passing note: I wrote a biographical Broadway play about another legendary entertainment figure, George Burns, and in researching it, I listened to countless radio broadcasts by Burns and Gracie Allen. Meredith Willson was their orchestra leader for a number of years, as he was on several other network radio shows and, as was the tradition of that time, he became a recur-ring comedic character (in this instance, almost a male equivalent of Gracie's giddy character). Meredith may have looked studious and unsophisticated, a potentially easy mark for a confidence artist such as Professor Harold Hill, but anyone who can hold their own comedically sharing a microphone with the likes of George Burns, Gracie Allen, Jack Benny and Tallulah Bankhead—as Willson did on a regular basis—is no naif.

Your tour guide in the volume ahead is the remarkable Mark Cabaniss and you can rest assured you are in the most knowledgeable hands for the enthralling story he will be sharing with you. Mark understands the world and evolution of *The Music Man* just as he has sweeping knowledge of every aspect of the entertainment field firsthand. He is himself a melodious composer, a savvy arranger, the creator of populist musicals many of which spring from the same neck of the woods and bend of the Mississippi as Mr. Willson's greatest work. He is an expert musical and theatrical historian to whom I've turned when I've needed an authoritative opinion or insight. He's a natural storyteller, and what follows (*lucky you, we're almost done with this part!*) is a tale rich with humanity, perseverance, vision, a little luck and one person's quest to entertain, divert and enlighten the world about life, love, childhood dreams and adult yearnings. Most of all—Wait, what's that I hear? Why, it's the Well Fargo wagon bearing something special, and it seems to be stopping here just for you. . . . Well don't just stand there gawping, read on!

Rupert Holmes*

*Rupert Holmes was the first individual in theatrical history to win solo Tony awards for book, music, and lyrics for his musical *The Mystery of Edwin Drood*, which also won that year's Tony award for Best Musical. He received the same honors from the New York Drama Desk and won in their additional category of Best Orchestration. He received a Drama Desk for his book for the musical *Curtains* with a score by Kander and Ebb, and a Tony nomination for Best Play for *Say Goodnight, Gracie.*

PROLOGUE

Against All Odds

Broadway musicals were a central feature of American pop culture in the 1950s. Some of the most beloved creations of the genre were born during that decade: *Guys and Dolls, South Pacific, Finian's Rainbow, My Fair Lady, The King and I, Once Upon a Mattress*, and *The Sound of Music* to name several. That list alone leaves one breathless in those shows' lasting impact on pop culture, let alone American musical theatre. It's no wonder that era comprised a large portion of what was the golden age of Broadway musicals.

Also in the 1950s was *The Music Man*. The year was 1957:

January 6: Elvis Presley appears on *The Ed Sullivan Show* for the third and final time.

February 4: The first nuclear-powered submarine logs its sixty-thousandth nautical mile, matching the endurance of the fictional *Nautilus* described in Jules Verne's novel *Twenty Thousand Leagues Under the Sea*.

March 31: Rodgers and Hammerstein's *Cinderella*, the team's only musical written especially for television, is telecast live by CBS-TV, starring Julie Andrews in the title role. More than 107 million viewers see the broadcast—a television record.

July 16: U.S. Marine Major John Glenn flies an F8U Supersonic jet from California to New York, setting a new transcontinental speed record.

August 5: *American Bandstand*, a local dance show produced in Philadelphia, joins the ABC Television Network.

August 21: President Dwight D. Eisenhower announces a two-year suspension of nuclear testing.

September 4: The Ford Motor Company introduces the Edsel on what the company proclaims as "E Day."

October 4: The first man-made satellite, the Soviet Union's *Sputnik*, is launched into space.

November 7: The Gaither Report calls for more American missiles and fallout shelters.

It was a slightly rainy day in New York City on Thursday, December 19, 1957, the day of *The Music Man*'s Broadway opening night. It was unseasonably warmer than average that day with a high temperature of 57 degrees.

The show had just finished its final out-of-town tryout in Philadelphia where star Robert Preston lost his voice during the run. But by the production's arrival to New York in trucks and cars and trains, Bob was back in fine form, while the show itself had experienced the usual bumps and bruises of rewrites and technical glitches in the run-up to Broadway. The show had been in development for several years, which included Meredith writing more than forty drafts and almost forty songs for a show that needed about twenty.

Their final preview performance in New York on Wednesday night proved to be a "disaster" according to Meredith. "No laughs, no tears, very little applause, and very few reactions," said Meredith, of the well-heeled audience that night who paid extra for tickets because it was a benefit performance. Such audiences are often reticent to love a show they feel is in their debt to live up to the extra bucks spent on tickets for "the cause."

By the time the curtain rose at 8:30 p.m. (the then-appointed curtain time for Broadway shows) the following, opening night at the Majestic Theatre, Meredith had given his special opening night gift to his wife, Rini (details later). He and Rini seated themselves in the farthest two seats on the side of the theatre under box seats nearest an exit. "Plenty of places to hide, easy to duck out fast," said Meredith. The fate of Meredith's musical was now out of his hands.

Meredith's cold hand with wet palm held Rini's cold hand with its wet palm on that opening night in 1957 as the show's overture began, and when the curtain came down approximately two and a half hours later, a miracle had happened. Against all odds, *The Music Man*—book, music, and lyrics all the creation of a Broadway novice from Iowa—with a star onstage who had never been in a musical comedy before, was a bona fide hit.

Cy Feuer (who was going to be the original producer of the show with his producing partner Ernie Martin, comprising the legendary producing team of Feuer and Martin) said, "That opening night audience sprang to its feet and clapped in rhythm to 'Seventy-Six Trombones' as the song triumphantly reprised during the curtain call"[1] (and such a joyous response has been repeated in every subsequent production it seems for more than sixty years).

The musical theatre canon is littered with flops that were created by writers and producing teams with successful track records, including Rodgers and Hammerstein, Stephen Sondheim, and Andrew Lloyd Webber, among others. That even greats Alan Jay Lerner and Charles Strouse had a real "stinker" with *Dance a Little Closer*, for example (closing after one performance), among their many other successful shows isn't unique. After all, creating a musical is one of the most difficult artistic endeavors one can tackle. And most musicals are up against substantial odds. But in the "odds category," based on what the Broadway intelligentsia said about *The Music Man* during its road to Broadway, if Las Vegas oddsmakers were handicapping the show's success or failure, the odds would have been 100 to 1 against its success. And the show (against such substantial odds) not only would succeed on Broadway but that it even came into being to begin with—and has continued for decades with no signs of slowing down—therein lies the miracle. It even went on to win the Best Musical Award over the critically acclaimed (and now also legendary) *West Side Story* in the 1958 Tony race.

This book is not intended as a "deep dive" into analyzing the music and lyrics of Meredith Willson, his shows, or the minutiae of his life. That has been done already by others. Instead, this book's purpose is to share the "essentials" of Meredith's personal story, the backstory and details of the musicals he wrote—especially *The Music Man*—enhanced in this book by those who knew him best, such as his wife Rosemary; his almost-producer, the legendary Cy Feuer; and others also personally interviewed: I connected with Eddie Hodges, *The Music Man*'s first Winthrop, and the only living principal cast member from the original Broadway production. Eddie was generous in his support and enthusiasm of this book. Finally, my time with Shirley Jones in her California home was a special treat never to be forgotten. Her love and fond memories of her time on the set of the Warner Bros. film version of *The Music Man* are entertaining and enlightening. She is truly as gracious and lovely in person as she is on the screen, and her contributions to this book are invaluable.

My time doing research at The Great American Songbook Foundation—where Meredith Willson's papers are housed—was thrilling and adds marvelously to this book. If meeting and visiting with Rosemary Willson in her and Meredith's home on several occasions wasn't enough, spending time connecting with countless photos and documents from Meredith's personal collection truly brought his fascinating and inspiring journey vividly to life for me.

This is the story of that hit musical with such odds against Meredith and his "lovely play" (as its producer, Kermit Bloomgarden, first called it). And it's the story of its inevitable creator himself. Plus, the alignment of talent, hard work, and good fortune that made (and makes) Meredith Willson known in many circles as "America's Music Man."

One

GOOD MORNING, RIVER CITY

I didn't have to make anything up for *The Music Man*. All I had to do was remember.

—Meredith Willson

It was another cold, wintry 1912 Sunday morning at 308 S. Pennsylvania Avenue (later re-named South Superior Street) in Mason City, Iowa. This sleepy town (1912 population was eleven thousand) was just waking up that morning when ten-year-old Meredith Willson came bounding down the stairs into the parlor to his mama, Rosalie, playing "The Church in the Wildwood" on the black upright piano. Smiling, Meredith started singing naturally and immediately along with the music. Rosalie nicknamed Meredith "Glory" because he always seemed to have a smile on his face. Older siblings, Dixie and Cedric, heard the fun and came to join in. But the fun couldn't last long because there were chores to be done, such as shoveling the fresh snow that had fallen overnight before going to Sunday school (where his mama taught) at the First Congregational Church a few blocks away. Meredith and Cedric would secretly try to figure out how to avoid going to church that day so they could go sledding after their chores. But mama and papa John would make sure all would be in attendance.

After church (or any day of the week) would be time for Meredith to practice his piano exercises. "If you're going to play an instrument," said mama, "you need to be good at it so as to stand out from the other boys."[1] Such piano practice always incorporated five-finger exercises, which often included a cross-hand move where the left hand crosses over and above the right hand on the keyboard to play an upper key (a move that Meredith would later incorporate in *The Music Man* for the next-door neighbor child, Amaryllis, who took piano from Marian the Librarian).

Before Meredith came bounding down those stairs that morning, he'd been born on May 18, 1902, in Mason City. At fourteen pounds, six ounces, he was the largest baby ever born in Iowa at the time. His brother, Cedric, was born in 1900 and sister, Dixie, in 1890. The Willsons endured the great sadness of having a second child—a baby girl—die in infancy.

Dixie played harp, Cedric the bassoon, and Meredith the flute. They all played piano because Rosalie taught it in their home. Meredith observed later in life that he found it curious and funny that it seemed most often in reference to teaching piano, piano teachers used the word "give" (not teach) piano lessons. And accordingly, their students "took" piano—unlike other instruments, where the teacher would "teach" lessons and students would "practice." So as Meredith says regarding kids taking piano, "My mother gave, so I had to take"[2] (whether he liked it or not). Fortunately, however, Meredith paid attention to his mama's music lessons.

Rosalie Willson also often directed the church Christmas cantatas and, of course, recruited young Meredith to participate. Meredith didn't like participating because his mama insisted that he wear black velvet pants, which made him feel a little too "stuffy" and proper. One of his earliest roles at the age of four was as a shepherd telling the Christmas story. As Meredith and three other shepherds approached a Bethlehem citizen to inquire about the bright shining star above Bethlehem, the citizen told them they should ask that of Joseph. But Joseph was nowhere to be found on stage. Showing his ability for a quick ad-lib, Meredith piped up and said, "The good father Joseph will be here in a minute. He hath gone to the toilet."[3] As the audience roared with laughter (and Rosalie and John probably turned red), something must have sparked inside that little four-year-old boy.

And the famous Star of Bethlehem, as far as the Mason City's First Congregational church was concerned, was created by a crude early twentieth-century contraption owned by church member Charlie Rau, the stereopticon. This early projector would make magic happen. Meredith recalled,

Charlie had painted the Star of Bethlehem on a slide and at Christmas time would point the machine in every direction to make the star travel across the ceiling of the church, down the wall, and finally end up over the choir loft. There Avis Stott would stand and sing "Joy to the World," combining glorious music, showmanship, and electrical magic enough to set my little four-year-old cork a-bobbin' with the first real thrill that I can remember.[4]

Church involvement stayed with Meredith throughout his life—concluding at the Westwood Hills Congregational Church in Los Angeles, where he was a member (and deacon) from 1948 until his death. He paid for a stained-glass window in the church, known as "The Music Man Window." It was placed above the pew where he and wife Rini (and after Rini's death, wife Rosemary) Willson sat. Rosemary remembered fondly the lovely stained-glass window, which "shows several different instruments in brilliant and beautiful colors."[5]

When he was six, after having been bitten by the performance bug, Meredith ventured outside the church walls for more performance opportunities. A few blocks from Meredith's home (and now where The Music Man Square also sits) was Mason City's Princess Theatre that put on little playlets prior to showing movies. Meredith somehow landed his first paying gig there (one penny for one performance) by agreeing to get inside a frog suit and hop up and down while biting on some wires to make the eyes glow on the suit. Right after his debut in this newfound secular theatre world, he made a beeline to the Candy Kitchen, where he immediately spent his hard-earned wages. With tears rolling down his cheeks, he immediately regretted the instant gratification of a single chocolate in exchange for a penny's worth of humiliation in a green frog suit. He had spent his newfound small fortune all at once in one place.

The United States in 1912

Legendary composer Marvin Hamlisch once said, "Meredith Willson is the only man who could have written *The Music Man*."[6] And for good reason. When you consider the era in which Willson grew up, his musical background, and the experiences he had long after childhood, you can't separate Meredith from this show.

It was Iowa in 1912 that Meredith chose to set *The Music Man*. He called the show his "valentine" to Iowa, and it's no wonder he chose that period for his musical because his formative childhood years were the basis for many of the characters, scenes, and tone that inform the show. For example, Meredith once wrote about certain sounds in that era in one of his books:

> Sounds stay in your memory longer than anything else, it seems to me. The older I get, the clearer I can hear the sounds that were the dimensions of the world during my first seven or eight years in it back in Mason City. Sounds like Mama scraping the burnt toast downstairs while you're hurrying in your "ironclad" stockings and your "underwaist"—that little harness affair with all the buttons on it. And the particular sound of your front door opening in the winter and the screen door slamming in the summer, and Papa's derby hitting the newel post in the front hall, almost a dead heat with the six o'clock whistle you could hear all the way from the roundhouse, and "The Toreador Song" on the music box while you had to take your afternoon nap.[7]

In the Midwest at the beginning of the twentieth century, there were no department stores or retail chains, just small, independently owned stores that specialized in various products. From hardware to shoes to hay and feed and other "fancy goods"(as one of the traveling salesmen calls such things in the opening number of *The Music Man*), these local stores were ripe for wholesalers that developed, offering far-away manufacturers' products to these mom-and-pop stores. And those wholesalers and manufacturers needed traveling salesmen to hawk their wares. But these traveling salesmen were suspect by local retailers and townsfolk because the salesmen were often displacing locally manufactured goods in place of others that would be shipped in (via train or Wells Fargo wagon), let alone introducing "new-fangled" goods in place of the tried-and-true products to which people were accustomed. And on top of it all, these salesmen were often selling directly to customers in their designated territories, cutting the local retailer out of the selling equation. And if that weren't enough, because the salesmen represented large companies with much deeper pockets than the local mom-and-pop retailers, they could offer their goods on credit.

When the cross-country rail system had been laid in the United States, these salesmen could now cover much more territory than before, including smaller towns that had henceforth been too difficult to reach economically. As the twentieth century dawned, there were hundreds of thousands of traveling salesmen across the country.

Although the innovative and ingenious train opening (titled "Rock Island," as in Rock Island, Illinois) from *The Music Man* seems inevitable now, it was anything but (more on that later). In retrospect, with the background of the life of a traveling salesman in the early 1900s, it's no wonder the patter is written as it is. As the curtain goes up on Act One, Scene One of the show, the salesmen state their plight, speaking in rhythm imitating the sounds of a steam locomotive:

> *1st Salesman:* Cash for the merchandise, cash for the button hooks.
>
> *3rd Salesman:* Cash for the cotton goods, cash for the hard goods.
>
> *1st Salesman:* Cash for the fancy goods,
>
> *2nd Salesman:* Cash for the noggins and the piggins and the firkins.
>
> *3rd Salesman:* Cash for the hogshead, cask and demijohn.
> Cash for the crackers and the pickles and the flypaper.
>
> *4th Salesman:* Look whatayatalk, whatayatalk, whatayatalk, whatayatalk, whatayatalk?
>
> *5th Salesman:* Wheredayagitit?[8]

Indeed, things were different in 1912 for traveling salesmen as they had been at the turn of the century. As a matter of fact, the year was significant in the life of the average traveling salesman because that was the year F. W. Woolworth was incorporated, which would eventually become one of the largest retail chains in the United States. Woolworth used a central buying approach to stock their stores, eliminating the need for traveling salesmen to sell local stores on their wares (and with their deep line of merchandise at attractive prices, Woolworth was driving many mom-and-pop stores out of business). To further rub salt in the traveling salesman's wounds, U.S. automakers were making new cars at a blistering pace in that era, many of which were Model T Fords. These cars made it easier for customers to travel outside of their immediate area to one of those regional glittering Woolworth stores. So one can understand the further complaining the salesmen continue with in "Rock Island":

3rd Salesman: Why it's the Model T Ford made the trouble,
Made the people wanna go, wanna get, wanna get,
Wanna get up and go seven, eight, nine, ten, twelve,
Fourteen, twenty-two, twenty-three miles to the county seat.

3rd Salesman: Who's gonna patronize a little bitty two-by-four kinda store anymore?

4th Salesman: Whaddaya talk, whaddaya talk,

3rd Salesman: Gone, gone
Gone with the hogshead cask and demijohn,
Gone with the sugar barrel pickle barrel, milk pan,
Gone with the tub and the pail and the tierce!

The salesmen's attention and patter then turns to a salesman who seems to be getting it right these days in such a challenging environment:

2nd Salesman: Ever meet a fellow by the name of Hill?

Charlie: Hill?

All But Charlie & 2nd Salesman: NO!

3rd Salesman: What's the fellow's line?

2nd Salesman: Never worries 'bout his line.

2nd Salesman: Or a doggone thing, he's just a bang beat, bell ringing,
Big haul, great go, neck-or-nothing, rip roarin',
Every time a bull's eye salesman,
That's Professor Harold Hill, Harold Hill.

Charlie: He's a fake, and he doesn't know the territory![9]

The next section of the number reveals just what this "bull's-eye salesman" has in his bag. Professor Harold Hill could have been the best kidney plaster or anvil salesman west of the Mississippi and been mopping up. But no, this traveling salesman was hawking something that was as popular at the time as apple pie: a boys' band.

> *2nd Salesman:* He's a music man.
>
> *1st Salesman:* He's a what?
>
> *2nd Salesman:* He's a music man and he sells clarinets
> To the kids in the town with the big trombones
> And the rat-a-tat drums, big brass bass, big brass bass,
> And the piccolo, the piccolo with uniforms, too
> With a shiny gold braid on the coat and a big red stripe runnin' . . .
>
> *1st Salesman:* Well, I don't know much about bands but I do know
> You can't make a living selling big trombones, no sir.
> Mandolin picks, perhaps and here and there a Jew's harp . . .
>
> *Second Salesman:* No, the fellow sells bands, Boys' bands.
> I don't know how he does it but he lives like a king
> And he dallies and he gathers and he plucks and he shines,
> And when the man dances certainly, boys, what else?
> The piper pays him! Yes sir, yes sir, yes sir, yes sir,
> When the man dances, certainly, boys, what else?
> The piper pays him! Yesssssir, yessssir.[10]

Bands across the Land

The earliest military marching bands that historians have documented were from the Ottoman Empire in the thirteenth century. The Ottomans conquered vast swaths of territory in Northern Africa, the Middle East, and Southern Europe and brought their marching band tradition with them. By the late 1700s, military bands were becoming a part of American culture, and by the mid-1800s, many towns large and small had their own marching bands for parades and other holidays and celebrations (especially July 4th activities).

These marching bands featured lots of brass and percussion, as well as wood-winds, and would eventually feature the sousaphone—a "portable" marching version of the concert tuba. The instrument was named for its inventor, the great bandmaster and composer John Philip Sousa (for whom Meredith would eventually play under his direction). These early bands accordingly became closely connected to patriotic activities, and like sports, became a method to promote moral and physical strength to young boys (for at the time, no girls were allowed). Today, marching bands still are strong in high schools, colleges, and universities . . . with schools such as Ohio State, the University of Southern California, the University of Tennessee, and Purdue University among the best. Meredith himself wrote "The Iowa Fight Song" in 1951 for the University of Iowa, which is sung to this day.

Professional "corps style" marching bands have flourished in the United States since the late 1970s. These bands are sanctioned by Drum Corps International (DCI). Where the military style is usually a constant forward march and may incorporate an abrupt turn or "about face," corps style incorporates forward, backward, and side-to-side marching. Military bands generally always face the end zone of a football field, whereas corps bands generally face the main audience (home-side press box). A significant break from the military tradition used in corps style is instead of baton twirlers, a color guard that is a separate unit, doing their own drill and routine. Often, corps-style color guards use multiple designs for silks during the show, as well as rifle and sabre. Musically, military bands perform marches. The corps style can incorporate any or multiple styles of music to fit the theme of their show. Corps-style bands can use props and backdrops to enhance the theatrical quality of their show, whereas military bands generally don't have a them for their shows.[11]

So in one fell swoop, the opening number "Rock Island" in *The Music Man* lays the foundation for what is to unfold before the audiences' eyes: The period in which the piece is set (Meredith's formative years), the need for, plight of, and logical suspicion of traveling salesmen of the day. Plus, the fact that one particular salesman is peddling boys' bands quite successfully. Yet, it is also revealed at the end of the number that Hill has been fleecing the citizens in towns he's visited and then promptly absconding with their money for instruments and a band that he never delivers. The salesmen pledge to catch up with

Hill someday (particularly one Charlie Cowell) and expose him as the fraud he is, therefore protecting the sacred fraternity and good reputation (at least, in their minds) of their profession. When the train comes to a grinding halt with an orchestra "button" to accent its arrival into "River City" (Mason City's alter ego)—Hill, who has been among the salesmen during the entire train ride, unbeknownst to them and the audience, jumps up and slickly escapes the train before they can catch him.

From the opening scene of the show, the audience knows that Harold Hill is a con artist. It's now up to Meredith to convince the audience why they should spend more than two hours with this charlatan—cheer for him to get the girl—and win over a skeptical town who would want to tar and feather him when they find out they've been had.

Quite a tall order for Meredith—taller than the Iowa corn that surrounds Professor Harold Hill when he bounces off that train into the hay and sarsaparilla belt of the Hawkeye State. And although Meredith didn't know the territory of Broadway, he surely could remember what a cold Iowa morning felt like when mama told him to shovel the snow and then practice his five-finger piano exercises.

Two

ALL IN THE FAMILY

Got to get mama into this show.

—Meredith Willson

The significance of ancestry and birth order is well-documented and an interesting and worthy study as to its impact on the dynamics of any family. Gender, age gap between children, number of children, and other factors certainly have an influence on the family and children involved. Considering Meredith Willson's grandparents and parents, followed by rewinding to Meredith Willson's Mason City days, it is also worth noting Meredith's siblings, as well as some of his parents' ups and downs. Although I won't attempt to analyze the impact family dynamics likely had on Meredith's destiny, it is instructive to lay out the facts for you to draw your own conclusions as to how those dynamics and twists of fate ultimately played a role in Meredith's fortunes. But there's no denying that Meredith Willson had a solid bloodline to help give him his musical foundations, solid work ethic, and pioneering spirit.

Alonzo Willson (b. 1822) was Meredith's grandfather. Born in Adams Center, New York, he married Catherine Reynolds in 1845 in Illinois, where Alonzo had moved to seek a better life. He became a farmer, but the challenges therein drove him to join the California gold rush in the mid-1850s to yet seek another "better life." Catherine stayed behind in Illinois while Alonzo chased the gold-rush dream. However, after two years, although things didn't "pan out" (pun intended) with gold nuggets for Alonzo, he did do some lucrative deals with gold miners resulting in amassing $10,000 in cash. Flush with cash, he was eager to return to Illinois, rejoin his wife, and continue building a family. But not long after returning, he was wooed to Iowa (specifically Cerro Gordo County) by a wealthy Iowa landowner, Anson Owen. Owen owned all the timberland in a place known as Owen's Grove (only a few miles from what eventually became named Mason City). Owen had heard of Alonzo's success and asked if Alonzo would like to purchase some of his land to farm. Not only did Alonzo jump at what looked like a great deal, but he also eventually ended up owning much of Owen's Grove due to his business acumen. Alonzo went on to oversee construction of the first school in the township and was its first teacher. In addition, he founded the first public library in Cerro Gordo County and was a justice of the peace. Alonzo and Catherine were true leading citizens and pioneers of their day.[1]

Alonzo and Catherine had a total of eight children, the youngest of whom was John (born in Iowa, unlike many of his older siblings who were born in Illinois). With John as the youngest of the brood, Emma was the oldest (and with the wide age difference among the eight children, Emma was biologically old enough to be John's mother). John was born in 1866 on the family farm in Owen's Grove. In 1878, Alonzo and Catherine moved their family to Mason City. The region around what was first called Shibboleth was a summer home to the Sioux and Winnebago nations. The town originally had several names: Shibboleth, Masonic Grove, and Masonville until Mason City was adopted in 1855, in honor of a founder's son, Mason Long.

The first settlement that became Shibboleth was established in 1853 at the confluence of the Winnebago River and Calmus Creek. Regarding creeks versus rivers in Mason City, Meredith wrote in "But He Doesn't Know the Territory":

> Mama liked nice-sounding words. Instead of ordinary ones like "creek." So Mama set about a good many years ago to prove that Willow Creek—a noble enough stream running beneath the South Superior Street bridge five houses south of our house—was not a creek at all but a river. Lime Creek on the other side of town was similarly unsatisfactory to Mama. Her efforts to provide these streams with official dignity embraced a lot of research and bales of correspondence proving among other things during the process why Mason City was settled where it was settled: Indians always located their villages at the confluence of two rivers—not creeks, *rivers*— thus, according to their belief, insuring peace and fertility. Well sir, the

Indian camp which became a village which became Owens Grove which
became Shibboleth which became Mason Grove which became Masonville which became Mason City was settled by Indians "at the confluence
of two rivers," said Mama. "Mason City is a River City, not a Creek City."[2]

So it was with great pride and some poetic justice that Meredith named the
fictional alter ego of Mason City in *The Music Man* "River City."

Although John Willson's earliest years were spent in Owen's Grove, his ado-
lescent years were spent in Mason City. When it came time to graduate from
Mason City High School, there were only six members in the graduating class.
Oddly enough, the city's board of education ruled to hold the small class over
for an additional year. John and the other five seniors balked at such an outra-
geous proposition and quit school. Not to be deterred in pursuing higher education, John convinced the admissions department at the University of Notre
Dame to admit him to a two-year law course. He completed the course and
then proceeded to take the Indiana state bar association exam. When it came
time for John to present before the state supreme court justices to pass the final
leg of the exam, he lied under oath about his age (he was shy of the minimum
legal age of twenty-one to practice law). John passed the bar.[3]

While John was attending Notre Dame, he was on the school's baseball
team. While playing an out-of-town game in Chicago, he was introduced
to Rosalie Reiniger, an 1881 graduate of Chicago's Armour Institute and the
daughter of a prominent attorney from Brighton, Illinois. Sparks flew and John
was determined to stay in touch with this lovely, cultured lady who always
seemed to appreciate the simple pleasures of life and "a few nice things" (an
idea that Meredith later incorporated into the lyric of "My White Knight" in
The Music Man):

> My white knight, not a Lancelot, nor an angel with wings
> Just someone to love me, who is not ashamed of a few nice things[4]

The couple married in 1889 at the Congregational church in Brighton. They
then moved to Estherville, Iowa, where John began a law practice and Rosalie became a primary school teacher and piano instructor. One of Meredith's

treasured memories of one of his mother's (funny) scrapbook clippings regarding her wedding from the local paper: "Prominent among the display of wedding gifts was a lovely combination pickle-dish and ink-stand."[5] Meredith goes on to write:

> There was a nice comment about the flowers, too. "The living room carried out a striking motif being decorated chiefly with syringes." How mama shrieked till she cried, laughing at that item. Got to get mama in this play, I thought almost every time I sat down to the typewriter [to write *The Music Man*].[6]

Life for the young couple in Estherville began in earnest. In addition to practicing law, John Willson played cornet and baritone horn with the Estherville band. One of the wedding gifts given to the new couple (in addition to the pickle-dish/ink-stand) was an upright grand rosewood piano, which Rosalie quickly put to good use as a piano teacher. John expanded his work to real estate and as a loan manager in addition to his law practice.

Rosalie Reiniger was accustomed to the legal world long before she married John. Her father, Gustavus Reiniger, was an attorney in Charles City, Iowa, and eventually became a federal judge. He also played flute for enjoyment in his spare time. He met and married Lida Meacham of Green Springs, Ohio, in 1857. In addition to Rosalie, Gustavus and Lida had three more daughters and a son. One of their daughters they named Lida.

While in Estherville, John and Rosalie had their first child in 1890, a girl, and named her Lucille (nicknamed "Dixie"). More on Dixie later. However, the young family's days in Estherville were numbered. Having spent his adolescence in Mason City, John was interested in returning with his bride to expand their family. Accordingly, in 1894, the Willsons moved to Mason City. Tragedy befell the Willsons when their second child, a daughter named Maurine, was born soon after moving to Mason City. Maurine contracted spinal meningitis at five months old and died on October 5, 1894. John Cedrick Willson ("Cedric") was born on October 26, 1900. Then, on May 18, 1902, their fourth child, Robert Meredith Willson, was born. (There were two more children noted as having been born sometime to John and Rosalie, but little is known about them other than they died in infancy.)

With Meredith's mama, named Rosalie ("Rose"), and his maternal grandmother and an aunt named Lida, it's no surprise he would later write a barbershop quartet song named "Lida Rose" for *The Music Man*.

Life in the Willson household on Superior Street in Mason City was strict and orderly, yet always busy, and especially full of music and often laughter. All three children played piano because Mama taught it. But according to Mama, for each child to "stand out from the rest" they should play another instrument.[7] So Dixie played harp; Cedric played bassoon; and Meredith the flute and eventually the piccolo (Grandpa Reiniger's flute-playing background might have been a subtle—or not-so-subtle—influence on Meredith's choice to play flute). Papa John played guitar and sang; Mama Rosalie piano. John also wrote poetry and maintained his love of baseball by playing on a local amateur team.

The Willson house on Superior Street (still standing—and restored now as a museum as Meredith Willson's boyhood home) had a parlor in the front of the house, where Rosalie gave piano lessons. Also on the first floor is a living room, dining room, and kitchen. The front door gives way to a staircase that

The Willson Home on Superior Street.
PHOTO COURTESY THE MASON CITY FOUNDATION. © THE MASON CITY FOUNDATION.

leads to a nursery and three bedrooms. The third floor was open space used as a playroom for their creative children's plays and other games.

While John was busy with his career, in addition to teaching piano, Rosalie taught Sunday school. At the end of each class, she would bid each of her young pupils goodbye with the words "May the good Lord bless and keep you." Meredith would later write a song using those words as its title. When he served as the music director on Tallulah Bankhead's *The Big Show* NBC radio program, she ended each show with the entire cast—weekly guest stars included—singing Meredith's "May the Good Lord Bless and Keep You." The song became an instant hit and was later recorded by a litany of stars, including Kate Smith, Perry Como, Bing Crosby, Liberace, Johnny Mathis, Cliff Richard, Tammy Wynette, and many more. Because of Rosalie's dedication to her church's educational department, she was named superintendent of the primary department (unheard of for a woman to head up such a department at the beginning of the twentieth century). In 1960, years after Rosalie had died, Meredith financed an education wing on the Mason City Congregational Church in her memory.

As a side note: I was invited to Mason City in the early 2000s by the Iowa Choral Directors Association to be one of their featured clinicians for their annual convention. Part of my duties at the convention was to conduct the conference choir through several numbers. I chose a choral arrangement of Meredith's "May the Good Lord Bless and Keep You" because the concert was to take place at the Mason City Congregational Church. After conducting the piece in that evening's concert, I went to the education wing of the church and Rosalie's old Sunday school class, after asking a church member to point me to it. Several people were milling about in the hall after the concert, and one lady wandered into the room to say hello and comment on the concert. I mentioned Rosalie's teaching in the room once upon a time, and the lady said simply, "May the good Lord bless and keep you." I smiled and thanked her, turned to survey the room further, and when I looked around, she was gone. I would like to think that lady was some ghostly spirit—even Rosalie herself—but her name tag read "Ginny." Perhaps Rosalie's ghost was *incognito*!

Rosalie was a lover of animals and founded the Mason City Humane Society. Additionally, she was a great supporter of the burgeoning kindergarten movement that was introduced in the United States at the time. She began an early education program in Mason City (which was after she had helped orga-nize the Chicago Free Kindergarten Association while she was a student at the Armour Institute). According to Meredith, "All the neighborhood kids loved Mama, because she treated them like individuals."[8] Therefore, the front porch of the Willson home became one of the favorite gathering places for all the neigh-borhood children so Mama could impart her wisdom and encouragement.

Dixie and Cedric

With the phenomenal success that Meredith enjoyed during his life, it's easy for his older siblings to possibly get lost in his shadow in retrospect. And perhaps there is some truth to that for Dixie and Cedric. But when examining their careers, one sees they were not underachievers to say the least. After all, they were born into an exceptional family of pioneers with a proud lineage.

Dixie Lucille Reiniger Willson became a screenwriter, as well as an author of children's books, novels, and short stories. She married a prominent Wis-consin businessman (whose father was elected to the U.S. Congress). However, their marriage could not ultimately survive both of their ambitions. Dixie had been writing stories and plays since her childhood and aspired to become a famous writer. Therefore, after a year of marriage, the two divorced amicably. Dixie packed her bags for Chicago, where she got a job as a dancer with a local theatre production. The show then transferred to Broadway, and she then landed in vaudeville and eventually as a Ziegfeld chorus girl.

Dixie eventually wrote numerous children's books, as well as many short stories and poems. Her best-selling children's book, titled *Honey Bear*, con-tains illustrations by Maginel Wright Barney, sister of famed architect/designer Frank Lloyd Wright. Novelist Tom Wolfe cites the book as the one his mother read to him at bedtime and first made him wish to be a writer.[9] Dixie was also a screenwriter; four of her screenplays were made into films (one of which was award-winning). She liked to gain firsthand experience when researching her stories and performed as an elephant rider in the Ringling Brothers Circus. She also attended TWA Stewardess School and worked as a taste tester at Betty Crocker. A colorful life, to say the least!

Like many siblings, Meredith and Dixie's relationship was not without complications. When *The Music Man* opened on Broadway, Dixie was sixty-seven
years old and, as noted, an accomplished writer in her own right. She gave
her brother kudos publicly for the immense success of the show and echoed
the Mason City *Globe-Gazette*'s comment that, "It couldn't happen to a nicer
man."[10] But in a private letter to a friend, she suggested that the idea for *The
Music Man* was indeed hers, and she had pictured Meredith playing the lead.
She went on to assert that she and Meredith had discussed the concept and
to collaborate on it.[11] However, those who were in on the earliest stages of the
development of the show firmly stood by Meredith and his creation and development and writing of it. Besides, Meredith was not averse to giving credit
where credit was due. In his book, *But He Doesn't Know the Territory*, he clearly
credits having met Franklin Lacey in San Diego, where the two hit it off and
proceeded to work diligently on shaping the basic storyline. Lacey (and now
his estate) has always received proper credit (and royalty remuneration) for his
important contribution to the show.

Dixie died in 1974 at the age of eighty-four. It isn't known for sure if Dixie
went to her grave holding a torch that she was somehow wronged as it regarded
The Music Man. But a stern rebuke in the form of a letter to Dixie is documented as having been written by then-longtime editor, Earl Hall, of the
Globe-Gazette in 1962, five years after *The Music Man*'s Broadway premiere.
Hall clearly makes the case, due to his firsthand experience during the development of the show and the facts, that Dixie's *Music Man* "theft" premise simply
wasn't plausible.[12]

Although Cedric Willson was also a fine musician, he never intended to
make it his lifelong profession. He was in the Sousa band with Meredith for a
time, but after his stint with Sousa, he went to the University of Kansas and was
awarded a degree in civil engineering. A master's degree in the same field followed from New York University. A twenty-five-year career with Texas Instruments followed, becoming a vice president. He rose to the heights of being
considered a top-notch expert in the field of lightweight aggregate concrete (of
all things). Back in the 1950s, the *New York Herald Tribune* had a tradition of
asking the writer of a new Broadway show to write an essay that would appear

in the paper on the eve of the show's opening. In the essay written by Meredith on the eve of *The Music Man*'s opening night, regarding his brother, he wrote:

> My brother is a very smart man in the industrial field. Light aggregate concrete. In fact, he is an expert. I don't mind telling that to you but that's the first time I've told it to him. That's what we call Iowa-stubborn.[13]

Although Cedric didn't enjoy the fame and accolades afforded Meredith and Dixie, he, too, had the same pioneer spirit fostered in that magical house on Superior Street in Mason City. He was part of the proud Willson tradition and nuclear family that had an impact far and wide. And Meredith was coming into his own to eventually create words and music that would be heard far beyond the walls of that three-story house in Mason City . . . and would resonate around the world for generations to come.

Three

MANHATTAN MAN

I began to feel my britches were getting too big for Mason City.

—Meredith Willson

Meredith Willson had worn many "britches" during his growing-up years in Mason City . . . from the black velvet pants in the church cantatas to his band uniform in the Mason City High School Band. But by the age of eighteen, Meredith knew he was ready for the next steps and to try his wings. He graduated from Mason City High School in 1919 and soon afterward, he boarded a train bound from Mason City to New York City. And in 1919, there was "only" a population gap between the two cities of more than ten million people. That was quite a potential culture shock for the young Hawkeye. To offer a proper send-off, Mama and Papa Willson were there to bid him farewell with their best wishes, along with the entire Mason City High School Band to play him off. Meredith said later in life that he left Mason City that day with "Papa's fried chicken, Mama's prayers, a mail-order flute, and a bent piccolo in his pocket."[1]

Meredith's wife, Rosemary, said, "Meredith never met a stranger. And he treated everyone alike . . . be they doctor, head of state, or janitor. His confidence was present even when he was so young and playing with the Sousa band. And that was one of the many things that served him well throughout his career."[2]

Meredith soon put his people skills to work in his new home. Not long after getting settled in his small apartment in New York City, Meredith made a connection with a fellow musician who pointed him in the direction of famed

Parisian flutist[3] Georges Barrère. After hearing Meredith play, Barrère immediately knew the young man had talent. Accordingly, Meredith soon began
taking private flute lessons from Barrère. And not only did Barrère teach pri-
vately, but he also taught at the prestigious Damrosch Institute of Musical Art
(founded in 1905 by Frank Damrosch). So Barrère also helped Meredith get
into Damrosch to become a student there. The Damrosch Institute eventually
became the Julliard School (to which Meredith would eventually donate—after
the success of *The Music Man*—millions of dollars to build The Meredith Willson Residence Hall). Barrère also knew how to advise up-and-coming musicians new to town on how to get playing gigs. His advice was to hang around
the local musician union hall and make connections with other musicians who
were working.

Ever the quick study, Meredith indeed started frequenting the union hall
where he met other young players. His New York City music networking had
therefore begun in earnest. Through his newfound connections, Meredith
soon met someone who asked if he could substitute for him at the Winter Garden, one of New York's most prestigious Broadway theatres. "My first paying
gig in NYC!" thought Meredith . . . and indeed it would be. He immediately

Georges Barrère.
PHOTO COURTESY LOS ANGELES
PUBLIC LIBRARY.

splurged on his meager financial resources and paid for a telegram home to Mama and Papa excitedly telling them of his subbing job. And off he went that night, carefully following the man's directions on how to get to the gig. When he arrived on Houston Street where he was told to go, he saw a "Winter Garden" alright, but it was the run-down Winter Garden burlesque house that sat atop a dingy market.

But a job is a job, thought Meredith. So in he went with his head held high to play. By the time he got back to his apartment that night well after midnight, he found a telegram tacked on his door from his parents that read: "Always knew you'd make good."[4]

But at least Meredith was off and running with a paying job, so more paying gigs possibly couldn't be too far away. And soon, indeed another (better) job came along playing at the Crescent Theater (a higher-level house), where Meredith made $52.50 a week. This helped him pay for the flute lessons with Barrère, as well as broaden his studies at the Damrosch Institute.

As Meredith worked steadily at the Crescent and other one-off gigs that would come along, he soon got his first big break six months after he'd arrived in New York: The great John Philip Sousa came calling and offered Meredith a full-time job as flutist in his band.

The Sousa Years

John Philip Sousa (1854–1932) was an American composer and conductor known primarily for U.S. military marches. He is known as "The March King" (writing more than 130 marches) or "The American March King" to distinguish him from his British counterpart, Kenneth J. Alford. Among his best-known marches are "The Stars and Stripes Forever," "Semper Fidelis," "The Liberty Bell," and "The Washington Post."

Sousa aided in the development of the sousaphone, which is a tuba that can be worn around the player's waist and shoulders while marching and playing. It is a modified helicon created in 1893 by Philadelphia instrument maker J. W. Pepper at Sousa's request, using several of his suggestions in its design. (Pepper evolved into what is today's largest print and digital music retailer, still based in greater Philadelphia.)

Sousa played in the Marine Band (also called "The President's Own" band) and then joined a theatrical pit orchestra, where he learned to conduct. This led to not just playing in the pit but also conducting pit orchestras. Probably his most celebrated job as a pit orchestra conductor was that for Gilbert & Sullivan's hit *H.M.S Pinafore* on Broadway in 1875. He eventually returned to the Marine Band as its head in 1880 and remained as its conductor until 1892. He led the band under five presidents, from Rutherford B. Hayes to Benjamin Harrison. His band played at the inaugural balls of James A. Garfield in 1881 and Benjamin Harrison in 1889.

Sousa organized the Sousa Band the year that he left the Marine Band, and it toured from 1892 to 1931 and performed at 15,623 concerts, both in the United States and around the world.

Many might have been instantly intimidated by meeting and playing for the great Sousa. And Meredith certainly had tremendous respect for Sousa—not only as a young man, but also throughout his life. Rosemary Willson explains Meredith's approach to meeting famous people:

> He was never intimidated when he met famous people. And he was never afraid to ask a dumb question for fear of being potentially embarrassed. He knew he would learn that way, and doors might open for him as he worked his way up through the ranks. And he had a gift also for remaining singularly focused on the task at hand and had the discipline to match.[5]

And now nineteen-year-old Meredith Willson was a part of this storied band—and he didn't even have to audition. That was because he came highly recommended to Sousa by Sousa Band cornet player Frank Simon. When the Sousa Band performed in Mason City in 1919, Simon had been introduced to the small town. Then, Simon returned a year later in 1920 as a guest soloist with the local municipal band. Part of Simon's duties with the Sousa Band was that of talent scout. He had heard about a young and talented local young man named Meredith Willson. So Simon sought Meredith out to hear him play. He was instantly impressed with Meredith's tone and overall musicianship and immediately recommended that Sousa sign Willson up. Sousa greatly valued Simon's opinion and judgment about talent and offered Meredith a contract.

(An aside about Simon: Years later, long after Meredith had written *The Music Man*, Meredith paid tribute to Simon in a letter to him writing, "I once wrote a song about 76 trombones and 110 cornets. This is a good time to reveal that there was only one cornet all the time . . . they just sounded like 110 cornets because you [Simon] were the cornetist.")[6]

Meredith toured the country with the Sousa Band for three years. Meredith found that Sousa ran a tight ship and that was just the sort of introduction to the music business that was the perfect foundation for the discipline he would exercise in the years to come as he continued to grow and blossom. For example, Sousa required his band members to always wear their uniforms in public. The uniform consisted of a starched white shirt, heavy coat, and pants. Sousa did allow band members to be out of uniform in mornings and the summertime (and later in his life, he relaxed the regulations to not wear uniforms during rehearsals). But the bottom line was that just as New York City eventually became the city that "if you can make it there, you can make it anywhere" according to the famous song lyric, so it was with Sousa's rehearsals. If you could get through the intensity of his rigid rules and rehearsals, you could get through just about any other ensemble. Thanks to Meredith's disciplined upbringing and his inherent strength of character and ambition, he was up to the challenge and passed with flying colors.

One of the hallmarks of a Sousa touring season ended with a concert at Madison Square Garden. It was such a celebrated event that even former Sousa band members would attend, wearing their old uniforms. And to end the concert—as Sousa ended all his concerts—was a stirring performance of Sousa's most famous march of all, "The Stars and Stripes Forever." The tradition on the final, glorious section of the march, which features the famous piccolo obbligato, was to have all the piccolo players in the band (which numbered around sixteen in any given season) come to the front of the band at the footlights and play their special obbligato. If the audience wasn't already on their feet by now, they always then jumped up and clapped in rhythm to the final flourish . . . then erupted into cheers. Add in twelve cornets, six trumpets, eight trombones, and four drummers and a variety of additional players (bringing the grand total to almost one hundred players), and the picture is clear. Certainly, such a moment was never lost nor forgotten by Meredith, and when he wrote the song "Seventy-Six Trombones" for *The Music Man*, one can clearly hear the influence of Sousa and those rousing concert moments:

> Seventy-six trombones led the big parade,
> With a hundred and ten cornets close at hand.
> They were followed by rows and rows,
> Of the finest virtuosos,
> The cream of every famous band.[7]

Meredith's career was off to a roaring start.

Sousa Band Concert poster.
PHOTO COURTESY NASHVILLE PUBLIC LIBRARY.

Meredith's years in the Sousa Band served him well, and vice versa. The *Philadelphia Record* singled out the young Willson in a 1922 review of the Sousa Band's performance. The music critic wrote the concert was particularly memorable because of a twenty-year-old flutist from Iowa. The columnist noted the solo in one of the pieces performed (Chaminade's "Concert in D") included a "difficult and delectable offering" from Willson. "The composition presents many difficulties, all disappearing before the musicianship of Willson."[8] But Meredith never rested on his laurels.

As noted previously, Meredith's brother, Cedric, also landed a spot in the Sousa Band. Years later, long after they had hung up their uniforms, they continued their connection with Sousa. By 1943, former band members started meeting for Sousa Band reunions to share "war stories" about their touring and playing lives on the road with Sousa, as well as Sousa himself. This eventually resulted in a formal organization (The Sousa Band Fraternal Society). Of course, both Meredith and Cedric joined. One member of the group was former flutist Jack Bell, who eventually played in the pit orchestra of *The Music Man* in its original Broadway production. And although Meredith, Cedric, and Jack were enthusiastic members of the society, it couldn't last forever as the Sousa Band members continued to pass away. Besides, Meredith—always looking forward—was eager for the next big thing. By ending his three-year tenure with Sousa, he was positioned for the next big thing—that of working with pioneer Dr. Lee de Forest, a fellow Hawkeye. De Forest was a US inventor and early pioneer in radio and in the development of sound-on-film recording used for motion pictures. A perfect foundation for the work Meredith would also eventually do with the great Charles Chaplin.

Four

FORWARD, MARCH!

I try to write about certain simple, sentimental facts of human beings that
are understandable and not discouraging and depressing.

—Meredith Willson

Thus far, according to this account of Meredith's life, you might think his
was a pretty charmed life. And although Meredith had skillfully taken
advantage of many opportunities given him, he had his share of "discouraging
and depressing" episodes in his childhood.

The John and Rosalie Willson family story was a great one—that of a successful, driven father and cultured, disciplined mother. And with three children
who were given a wonderful, foundational, and well-rounded childhood and
who were seemingly destined for success, these were the elements that made for
a perfect, storybook plot. But no great story is without a compelling or compli-
cating subplot, and the Willson family was not without such a substantial one.

Although the Willson home on South Superior Street was filled with a lot
of music, it was evidently also filled with a lot of arguments and strife between
John and Rosalie, at least eventually, in their union. After decades of marriage,
John and Rosalie ultimately discovered they were completely incompatible;
accordingly, they separated. Not long after they had separated, John wrote a
harsh and bitter letter to his wife. Here are excerpts from the letter:

> Rose:
> For the past twenty-five [sic] years, it has been plain to me, and probably to
> you, that we are a mismatched couple. Our view of life is so diametrically

opposed [sic] that no harmony has been, or can be possible, except by keeping away from one another. In view of the fact that we have three children, whose future has been a claim upon us, I have stayed with you and done the best I could to help rear them to manhood and womanhood.

I regret that the children have had to listen to [sic] disagreeable and inharmonious conversations, and have naturally acquired a querulous demeanor that will handicap them in life. As you are, you are to me as a red rag is to a bull, and it is nothing short of a crime for me to continue to ruin your life and for you to ruin mine as we have been doing for the past years.[1]

After thirty-one years of marriage, John and Rosalie divorced on February 5, 1920. Rose filed for and was granted the divorce on the grounds of "cruel and inhuman treatment." She also said that John was often away from home too much.

No sooner were John and Rosalie divorced than John (the same year of their divorce) married Minnie H. Hartzfeldt, a woman four years younger than his daughter, Dixie. Although in his bitter letter to Rosalie he'd claimed he would move across the state to start a new life, he and Minnie settled in a neighborhood one block behind his former family home. Rosalie planted tall shrubs to block the view of their home. She never remarried and proceeded to refer to herself as a widow for the rest of her life.

Although Meredith repeatedly wrote (and spoke) about his family upbringing and school days with great enthusiasm and affection in all his writings, he almost never described any dark and negative emotions and memories. That's probably due to the positive and hopeful attitude and outlook that pervaded Meredith's life. Regarding his parents, he never wrote of what must have been a painful situation for the entire family, let alone his parents' actual divorce. And he rarely mentioned his father in his writings. That inevitably stemmed from being shunned by his father. In a 1970 interview with the *Washington Star* at age sixty-eight, Meredith shared his feelings in one of the rare times one can find anything he said on the record about his relationship with his father:

My mother and father already had a son and daughter, Cedric and Dixie. They were the apples of my father's eye. He was angry when my mother told him I was on the way. From that time on, my father never spoke directly to my mother by name and never in my lifetime did I hear my name pass through my father's lips.[2]

But Meredith evidently never stopped longing for and seeking his father's approval, respect, and love. Meredith went on in the *Star* interview and described the time his father was at the famed Mayo Clinic in Rochester, Minnesota, being treated for an illness. The Sousa Band had a concert in a nearby town, and Meredith made a point to visit his ailing father.

> I stopped in to see him and told him I was first flute with the Sousa band and playing a solo each day and maybe he'd like to hear me. I stood in that hospital room and played for him and he still wouldn't admit he appreciated it or I was talented or I was good at anything. I really think I sped his demise. That was the last time I saw him alive.[3]

This was obviously a heartbreaking account of his relationship with his father, and one can only imagine the moments of pain and insecurity it must have caused him at times during his life. His mama, however, balanced out the deficit he experienced with his father. Rosalie clearly had a substantial and positive influence on Meredith's life. And with her strong influence on his life helping instill in him focus, achievement, and self-discipline, Meredith was able to say "forward, march!" with his life to move ahead. Meredith obviously overcame it all and (perhaps partially because of it) succeeded despite his father's lack of support (and success at a level possibly surpassing even Meredith's own wildest dreams). Because of the strife between his parents coupled with his drive to succeed, it's no wonder that he left town the first chance he had upon his high school graduation to move to New York City to pursue his dreams.

Early Wedding Bells

One vital fact regarding Meredith's personal life during this era has yet to be revealed in this account: Approximately a year after Meredith left Mason City for New York, he returned to marry his childhood sweetheart, Elizabeth "Peggy" Wilson (yes, she was also a Wilson, though with one "L"). Meredith even commented in the "Line Most Proficient In" section of his high school annual *The Masonian*, he would someday be "consolidating Wilsons."[4] Possibly to keep things simple or because of Meredith's parents' marital problems at the time, they eloped (to Albert Lea, Minnesota, thirty miles north of Mason City). Meredith—at the young age of eighteen—and Peggy married on August 29, 1920, the same year John and Rosalie had divorced. After tying the knot, Meredith returned to New York with his new bride to continue his education and matriculation into New York as a gigging musician. Meredith and Peggy would remain married for twenty-six years and, according to Peggy, divorced eventually because of Meredith's hectic travel schedule. On what would have been the couple's fiftieth wedding anniversary, with the approval of his then wife, Rosemary, Meredith made a magnanimous gesture and sent Peggy flowers.[5]

As Peggy pursued a teaching degree from the Ethical Cultural School in New York, Meredith continued to naturally network and connect with fellow musicians. He landed a job as flutist in the Times Square Rialto Theatre orchestra, and it was during that time, he was introduced to fellow Iowa native, Dr. Lee de Forest. De Forest was an inventor and early pioneer in radio and the development of sound-on-film recording used for motion pictures. At this point in the film industry, motion pictures were still silent, and the era of "the talkies" hadn't arrived yet. The only way for music to accompany a film was to have a pit orchestra, piano player, or organist accompany the film to underscore the action with music. De Forest experimented with what he called the "Phonofilm" process, wherein sound was recorded on film in light waves "married" alongside the picture on a print. De Forest took a liking to the young Hawkeye, was impressed with his talent, and signed Meredith up to play flute for his experiments. De Forest was awarded several patents that led to the first optical sound-on-film technology with commercial application. Over a four-year period, he improved his system with the help of equipment and patents licensed from another inventor in the field, Theodore Case. Meredith's important association with de Forest in the film industry only whetted his appetite for later contributions to the medium through not only his stage scores that were adapted for film but also contributing the scores for two major Hollywood productions, *The Little Foxes* and Charles Chaplin's *The Great Dictator* (more on those films later).

As Meredith dutifully supported his wife, played in the Rialto Theatre orchestra, and played other miscellaneous gigs as they were offered, he tried his hand at his first important classical work. The result was *Parade Fantastique*, which was soundly thumped by the critics. However, the composition was published. But when Meredith showed up to the publisher's office several months after its release, eager to be paid his royalty due for the work, due to the low performances of the piece he merely received pocket change and was promptly shown the door. But there was ultimately a happy ending to this *Parade*, in that it was originally premiered by the New York Philharmonic. This led to Meredith being noticed not so much as a composer at that time due to the premiere, but his musicianship as a flutist came to the attention of the philharmonic. So, in the fall of 1924, he joined the flute section of this premiere orchestra, leaving his Rialto days behind. Joining the New York Philharmonic during this era meant to play under the baton of the intense and fierce Arturo Toscanini. Meredith had just made a quantum leap in his young career.

Terrific and Terrifying Toscanini

Italian conductor Arturo Toscanini was one of the most acclaimed and influential musicians of the late nineteenth and early twentieth centuries, renowned for his intensity, his perfectionism, his ear for orchestral detail and sonority, and his photographic memory. Later in his career, he was the first music director of the NBC Symphony Orchestra, and that led to him becoming a household name (especially in the United States) through his radio and television broadcasts and many recordings of operatic and symphonic repertoire.

Rehearsals and performances under Toscanini's direction were rigid and disciplined, not completely unlike what Meredith had experienced working under John Philip Sousa. Although Meredith had certainly been exposed to a wealth of classical music prior to his tenure with the New York Philharmonic, this new position exposed him to a greater depth of the classics. The music of Mozart, Bach, Brahms, Weber, Respighi, Strauss, and Dvorak were now a regular diet for Meredith (and he later incorporated many of these classical composers' music in his future radio programs).

There's no question Meredith's early musical education and then making a living as a classically trained musician had an influence on his composing. Not only did he eventually compose many so-called serious (classical) works in his career, but many of his compositions for Broadway also incorporated ingenious counterpoint, the complexity of which is often found in classical music.

For example, in *The Music Man*, the songs "Lida Rose" and "Will I Ever Tell You?" are sung together, in counterpoint fashion, creating a unique moment in the show.

As the New York Philharmonic enjoyed healthy success and growth at this time, likewise so were other orchestras enjoying success and growth around the United States. And as those orchestras grew and began to flourish, so did the need for conductors and guest conductors of those organizations. After five years under the baton of Toscanini, Meredith's career began to branch out because he was invited to fill in as guest conductor for the American Philharmonic Orchestra in Seattle in 1929. The orchestra was a result of the new American Broadcast System (not to be confused with the later founded American Broadcast Company, ABC) opening a new studio in Seattle and sponsoring the orchestra as a means to help find new artists for the budding network. With his New York symphonic connections, Meredith was an attractive catch for the American Philharmonic even as a guest conductor. After all, the Mason City *Globe-Gazette* referred to Meredith in those days as a "young sensation" and "local prodigy."[6] And at age twenty-six, Meredith was called "the youngest philharmonic concert master in America" by the *Seattle Times*. Accordingly, anticipation was high when Meredith and Peggy stepped off the plane for his twenty-week guesting gig with the new American Philharmonic. But before he and Peggy departed New York, Meredith had convinced a dozen of his New York musician player friends to join him in this new adventure. To raise the stakes even higher, with his sights set on the conducting world, Meredith had resigned his position with the New York Philharmonic.

But according to Meredith, "We laid a very large egg in the shadow of Mount Ranier."[7]

The Seattle weather didn't cooperate, and torrential rains during that summer turned the audience "cold and gloomy" according to Meredith. Financial problems mounted with the orchestra and radio network, and both fledgling ventures soon failed, becoming little more than a footnote in Meredith's career. The plot had thickened in his life, with the challenges mounting as he and Peggy returned to New York.

Meredith remembered advice he had received from Sousa at one point when he told Sousa he was moving into conducting: "Keep your instrument handy."[8] So with his instrument handy, he procured any and all playing gigs to make ends meet. Many of them were public, and he inevitably ran into many of the musicians whom he'd recruited to play in the Seattle venue that summer. One such job was in a band playing in Central Park, which required he wear some sort of formal uniform, so he donned his old Sousa uniform. The irony wasn't lost on Meredith when, according to him, he ran into Sousa himself and Sousa was surprised to see Meredith back in town (as Meredith had told his old boss about his promising summer position in Seattle, which he hoped would lead to a full-time orchestra conducting position). Likewise caught by surprise and somewhat embarrassed at seeing Sousa, Meredith ad-libbed and told Sousa he was conducting an orchestra in Central Park (not just playing in it). Thinking not much of it, they bid farewell. Little did Meredith know that Sousa would show up to the concert that night. And when the concert closed with Sousa's own "The Stars and Stripes Forever," in the tradition, the piccolo players marched forward to play in formation in front of the orchestra. According to Meredith's account of that moment, as he played that famous obbligato, he happened to see in the front row none other than Sousa himself. Their eyes met. "And there I stood with my piccolo," wrote Meredith.[9]

Another forward, march moment it was for Meredith whether he was ready or not. Not unlike the real-life irrepressible heroine Molly Brown, whom Meredith would build a Broadway show around someday, Meredith was learning how to be "unsinkable." Accordingly, it was time for him to reinvent himself . . . again.

Five

ON THE AIR

If we have a duty, it is to give people some thread of hope, some kind of reassurance. The greatest single reassurances are in the world of art.

—Meredith Willson

After "laying a very large egg" in the shadow of Seattle's Mount Ranier (as Meredith put it) for the Seattle conducting gig, Meredith got busy trying to move forward. As he said at this point and on many occasions, "If you're a flute player you can always fall back on your pucker."[1] And before returning to New York temporarily to try to generate some cash, falling back on his pucker is precisely what he did. Nothing would keep him from pursuing his dreams, even if he felt as if he was going backward at times. As Rosemary Willson said regarding Meredith's philosophy in pursuing his dreams (let alone remaining solvent during lean times):

> If you're interested in something and want to pursue it and happen to then be in the right place at the right time, then you're able to move forward with it when your interest connects with opportunity.[2]

From the time he was a child in Mason City when he was dreaming of the next big thing at the Princess Theatre (which led to him dressing up in a frog suit for a play) to what his next move would be in Seattle, Meredith always was singularly focused on pursuing his dreams, even if it meant pulling out his flute again. Accordingly, Meredith landed a brief gig at Seattle's KJR radio station playing flute, which led to him eventually becoming the station's musical director. This radio experience would come in handy later, when radio became Meredith's chief form of supporting himself.

Meredith thought he had hitched his star to the right wagon with KJR because its executives envisioned "going national" with a coast-to-coast radio network, which would begin on the West Coast and spread nationally eventually. A small bit of momentum was achieved, but unfortunately the envisioned success never happened with the fledgling network, which soon shuttered.

To help continue making ends meet, Meredith was writing music for whatever medium he could find. Regarding his composing, Meredith once stated, "I had become a composer because I could never play the piano very well and it was embarrassing to just sit there."[3] Well, it obviously worked because Willson was a published composer (as noted previously) thanks to the his old friend Abe Meyer, who had relocated to Hollywood as head of the music department of an independent film production company, Tiffany Productions. This production company's most significant film to date had been *Peacock Alley* (1922), a silent film featuring film star Mae Murray (called "The Gardenia of the Screen," of all things). The film was such a hit, when "talkies" came along, it made sense for Tiffany to remake the film with the new sound technology (and with his previous work with Lee de Forest, Meredith had helped lay the foundations for the talkies). So when Meredith stopped by to see his old friend Meyer one afternoon as he was casting about for the next thing following the proposed new radio network's flop, interest indeed intersected with opportunity. Meyer asked Meredith to score the music for the sound version of *Peacock Alley*, which Meredith happily and eagerly accepted (although he had no experience scoring music for a film . . . but then, hardly anyone did in Hollywood in those early days of sound films).

The 1929 film was intended to be a comeback vehicle for Murray because her career had declined after she was unofficially blacklisted by Louis B. Mayer after she walked out on her MGM contract in 1927. Unlike the silent version, the sound remake of the film did not boost Murray's (or Meredith's) career and earned mostly unfavorable reviews. *Photoplay* called the film "a sorry affair," and Murray's performance "affected." The magazine went on to state, "You'll laugh at the drama and weep over the comedy."[4]

Not to be deterred, Meredith hitched up his bootstraps once again. Meyer and Tiffany Productions approached Meredith a second time later that same year to score another of their new talking films. This time, the assignment was *The Lost Zeppelin*, a fictional story about a naval officer modeled on U.S. Navy Commander Richard Evelyn Byrd, who was then a national aviation hero.

Lightning struck twice in a bad way with Tiffany, Meyer, and Meredith—the film was another flop. The *New York Times* gave a mostly negative review stating, "Presumably the producers of *The Lost Zeppelin*, an audible pictorial melodrama, do not believe in a very high order of intelligence among cinema audiences, for the best that can be said of the film is that it appears to have been fashioned with a view to appealing to boys from eight to ten years of age."[5]

Timing Is Everything

Meredith's radio and film connections, along with his talent and natural ability to communicate and network, paid off once again to propel him to his next project. On a trip to San Francisco from Seattle as he was looking for work (and to see a football game), he reconnected with one of his friends from Seattle, Merle Matthews, who had since relocated to San Francisco. Matthews was employed by San Francisco radio station KFRC, owned by entrepreneur Don Lee. Matthews introduced Meredith to Lee, and the two hit it off. Lee asked Meredith to create music arrangements for this leading West Coast radio station, to which Meredith happily obliged. This led to him eventually being named music director for the station and a relocation to San Francisco for Meredith and Peggy.

Again, Meredith was in the right place at the right time. The late 1920s through the late 1930s was a time of innovation and amazing growth for radio in general, and San Francisco became a pivotal and crucial hub in that development process. NBC and CBS opened West Coast divisions in San Francisco. Because new original programming was needed to fill the network schedules, the fledgling networks often relied on the creative pool in their West Coast divisions to fill the bill. Such programs would be broadcast throughout the western United States (a true simultaneous national network wasn't possible at this time in history because telephone lines hadn't been installed beyond the Rocky Mountains, so there were separate networks on each section of the United States—west and east—though they shared programming). Meredith was not only writing original music plus theme songs for such programs in his role at KFRC but was also often having that music published. For example, his published 1933 song "Show Us the Way, Blue Eagle" was born on a radio show and used the American eagle as a symbol of hope in the song to inspire and encourage a country mired in the Great Depression. One of his biggest early radio hits was "The House of Melody," a song written with music by Meredith and lyrics by fellow radio personality John Nesbitt (subsequently published by San Francisco publisher Sherman, Clay & Co.). "The House of Melody" was written as a theme song for a radio show of the same name for which Meredith and Nesbitt cohosted.

Another show Meredith developed while at KFRC was called *The Big Ten*, where his orchestra played that week's ten most popular songs as measured by the show biz trade magazine *Variety*. Countdown music shows on radio and television nowadays are an old concept, but in the 1930s there was nothing on the air like *The Big Ten*. With this show, however, Meredith truly learned the old cliché that "imitation is the sincerest form of flattery" when the *Lucky Strike Hit Parade* aired back East on NBC. Seems an ad executive from New York heard Meredith's show on a trip to San Francisco, loved the idea, and proceeded to share the concept with NBC, which promptly created their own version of *The Big Ten*. *Lucky Strike Hit Parade* eventually became *Your Hit Parade*, and the rest is history, with it airing from 1935 to 1954 on radio and from 1950 to 1959 on television.

This was clearly a productive time for Meredith, and San Francisco captured his heart. "San Francisco has more personality than any other city I've ever been in," Meredith said, adding, "It's big, good, kind, and friendly."[6] Rosemary Willson stated:

> Meredith fell in love with San Francisco. He was very happy with the creative opportunities it offered him. He found that after the Seattle ups-and-downs he experienced, things seemed to be falling into place for him in San Francisco. His career in radio was really taking off.[7]

In addition to *The House of Melody* program, Meredith worked on several other shows at KFRC, including *Carefree Carnival, Saturday Nights, The Heckler Surprise Party, America Sings, The Wandering Minstrel, Waltz Time, Chiffon Jazz,* and *Concert in Rhythm.* Although he had no formal training in broadcasting, he was, in essence, earning bachelor's, master's, and doctoral degrees in radio production and performance due to his extensive work in this area.

Meredith loved San Francisco so much that the first symphony he wrote was titled *Symphony No. 1 in F Minor—A Symphony of San Francisco.*

> The inspiration [for his first symphony] came from glancing out of his twenty-second floor office in the Hunter Dublin Building on Sutter Street to the San Francisco Bay and the circle that would be closed when The Golden Gate Bridge was completed. He later recalled that the final notes of his *Symphony Number One in F Minor* or *A Symphony of San Francisco* emerged at about the same time as the great cables and rivets completed a masterpiece of American engineering. He also related that, even though the symphony and the bridge were finished at virtually the same time, the bridge "made more money."[8]

His symphonic work premiered at San Francisco's War Memorial Opera House in 1936, conducted by Meredith himself. In addition to some positive notices for the work and its composer/conductor ("[Willson is] handsome and charming and enormously gifted,"[9] wrote the *San Francisco Chronicle*), there were some mixed reviews as well. The work has endured, however, with performances occasionally through the many years since its premiere. His work received enough encouraging notices so as to fuel him to write *Symphony No. 2 in E minor—The Missions of California.* Although there were some positive notices about this work, it didn't receive as many favorable reviews as did his first symphonic work. But despite any mixed reviews for these early major works, the young composer/broadcaster was continuing to refine his skills and building a fine reputation while broadening his already rich network of contacts.

Meanwhile, the radio business was continuing to grow and expand on the West Coast. Los Angeles and Hollywood were now coming on strong in their own right to rival San Francisco (and New York City, for that matter) as a hub of radio production. After all, thanks to the film industry, Hollywood was loaded with acting and producing talent, so it was a natural and gradual migration to Hollywood that occurred. NBC had built a shiny new, state-of-the-art studio in Hollywood (CBS would soon follow with their own), further signaling the network's belief and investment into Los Angeles as the future home of their broadcast productions. Accordingly, Meredith was tapped to help in Los Angeles. Then, another big break in radio came for him.

Have Some Coffee with Your Jell-O

Maxwell House Showboat was a long-running, number-one hit show on NBC Radio airing every Thursday night. The program was sponsored by Maxwell House coffee, and it was inspired by the success of the successful Jerome Kern and Oscar Hammerstein Broadway musical *Show Boat*. As an additional tip of the hat to the Broadway show, it was hosted by Charles Winninger, who played the lead role of Cap'n Andy in the original Broadway production of the musical and the first film version of the show. The producers decided to move the program from its original production location of New York to Los Angeles, but the show's music director chose not to move with it. A call was put out to the man who had become a popular and successful West Coast radio music director and radio personality, Meredith Willson, to see if he might take the job. According to Rosemary Willson, Meredith said yes to the job "faster than an Iowa farmer could shuck corn."[10] And yet, Meredith accepted with mixed emotions because this meant he and Peggy would need to relocate to Los Angeles, leaving his beloved San Francisco behind. He said, "There must have been gloomy days when I lived there, but I don't remember them."[11]

 Maxwell House Showboat opened each week's broadcast with a paddle-wheel sound effect with a calliope and then the chorus and the orchestra: "Here comes the show boat, here's comes the show boat, puff puff puff puffin' along!"[12] Meredith writes about the opening night of the new Los Angeles–based production, starring Charles Winninger with Hattie McDaniel:

> That opening night, the studio clock was a minute and a half slow, so we
> were actually on the air a minute and a half before anybody realized it

except the engineer, who frantically signaled from the booth, but nobody saw him except the sound-effects man. So the long-awaited, glamorous *Hollywood Show Boat* opened up . . . accompanied by a few confusing remarks: "Good luck, Charlie old boy," "Give 'em hell, Hattie," "Well, this is it, kid, all the best." It sure was funny, or at least it is now to look back on.[13]

Meredith's time with *Maxwell House Showboat* served him well as he continued to gain valuable production experience and on-air exposure on the number-one network radio show. The Hollywood version of the show was a milestone in radio entertainment and ran for two years (not quite as long as expected, however). Then the "puff puffing" showboat ran out of steam. But Meredith wasn't in the unemployment line. Instead, he transitioned to the next big show that would also eventually become the number-one radio show in the United States. That show was *Good News*.

Also sponsored by Maxwell House (General Foods), *Good News* was notable as marking the first time a national network partnered with a major film studio (MGM) to create a show for sale to a commercial sponsor.

Jimmy Stewart was the program's initial host, with Robert Taylor then Robert Young following. By the fall of 1939, a variety of MGM stars filled in as hosts, with Dick Powell serving as the final host in 1940. Stars such as Frank Morgan, Fanny Brice, and Judy Garland also appeared. "The MGM Chorus and Orchestra" were conducted by Meredith. Meredith commented regarding the premiere broadcast of the show:

> MGM had taken over what is now the Paramount Theatre across the street from the Hollywood Hotel and rebuilt the stage into a replica of the Old Maxwell House in Nashville, complete with a crystal chandelier and forty or fifty thousand dollars' worth of gates and prop butlers serving Maxwell House coffee. We had lots of glamour and had rehearsed for many days with a big orchestra and chorus of seventy people and Jimmy Stewart, Jeanette MacDonald, Sophie Tucker, and Allan Jones and Judy Garland.[14]

Good News lasted until July 25, 1940. As the years changed, so did the title, becoming *Good News of 1939* and *Good News of 1940*. In its last few months on the air, it was known as *Maxwell House Coffee Time*. And as the old Maxwell house advertising slogan said, "good to the last drop," so was *Good News*—staying on top until Maxwell House and MGM decided to amicably part ways. But in the process of musically directing two back-to-back hit radio shows, Meredith had become a nationally known and bankable talent through his radio work and published compositions. His move to Los Angeles had truly paid off, and his dreams were coming true as time kept marching on. And then, another career breakthrough happened for him when he was asked by NBC to become musical director of their entire West Coast division.

Jumping ahead to 1948, Meredith was tapped to cook up a creative opening for Jell-O, sponsor of NBC radio's *The Aldrich Family*, starring Ezra Stone. The first two minutes of the show on October 21 introduced Meredith's "Talking People" in which five of Meredith's favorite singers—Norma Zimmer, Betty Allen, Maxwell Smith, John Rarig, and Bob Hanlon—spoke in unison as one individual. The result was rhythmic, electric, hilarious, and highly creative, and probably sold a lot of Jell-O in the process. This rhythmic speaking was clearly a forerunner of his opening train number in *The Music Man*—let alone the machine-gun rapid-fire oration of "Ya Got Trouble" also in the show.

Meredith's egg-laying days seemed to be over . . . at least for now.

Six

THE FABULOUS FORTIES

Imagination means nothing without doing.

—Charles Chaplin

During the 1940s, in which Meredith turned age forty in 1942, Meredith's career in radio continued to skyrocket, leading to even more professional opportunities—even when it was interrupted by a war.

As *Good News* was wrapping up in 1940, Meredith appeared on an episode of NBC's hit show *Fibber McGee & Molly*. And then, as *Fibber* was readying for its summer hiatus, it was announced that *Meredith Willson's Musical Revue* would be the show's summer replacement. Sponsored by Johnson's Wax, the show was loaded with music conducted and performed by Meredith's orchestra and singers. But as a fun gimmick, the titles of each song weren't announced before they were performed so that the audience would eventually guess the song titles. On top of that mystery touch, lyrics that might indicate the song title were replaced with "la, la, la, la" to completely obscure the song titles (somewhat of a forerunner to *Name That Tune*, a popular television show that would appear decades later).

Another unique aspect of the show as Meredith creatively played with music was his combining of one existing song simultaneously with another into a unified whole. For example, on *Meredith Willson's Musical Revue* on July 30, 1940, his orchestra played the hit song "Somebody Stole My Gal" followed by snippets of several classical pieces. Then, he put both segments together and *voila*, they fit together like a glove, creating a new music "taste" having combined the melodies together. This technique became later known in music circles as a "partner song," and Meredith seemed to particularly enjoy this technique, which he perfected on this show. He used the technique successfully later in *The Music Man* with the song "Lida Rose and Will I Ever Tell You?" For that (now iconic) moment in the show, as the barbershop quartet comes sauntering down the street on a summer evening and breaks into a love song ("Lida Rose"), Marian the Librarian (sitting on the porch, hearing the quartet) then segues into singing "Will I Ever Tell You?" contemplating a love interest. And then (as Meredith says in his 1959 Capitol Records recording *And Then I Wrote* The Music Man), "the inevitable happens"[1]: The barbershop quartet and Miss Marian combine their melodies, simultaneously creating a satisfying new combination, as Mother Paroo rocks peacefully in rhythm on the porch.

Meredith used this technique again in *The Music Man*, but unfortunately, it never made it into the final draft of the show. Thanks to Meredith's ingenuity, the melody for the song "The Sadder But Wiser Girl" (an up-tempo character song) can be superimposed over the melody for the song "My White Knight" (a soaring ballad). The former is sung by Harold Hill in Act One as he opines how he will never fall for a "wide-eyed, wholesome" type; the latter is sung by Marian as she opines what she is looking for in a husband, and that is *not* a fly-by-night Harold Hill–salesman type. That these two musically and textually contrasting songs can be sung perfectly together was intended to show that although these two characters in the show are at opposites at first, by the end of the show they (and we) discover they actually have much more in common than meets the eye. Meredith and his then wife, Rini (more on Rini later) perform this simultaneous pairing of the two songs on the *And Then I Wrote* The Music Man recording with amazing effect. It's worth tracking down the recording at a used record store or online if only to hear this one partner song as never before.

But Meredith did achieve the mission of musically showing the audience Marian and Harold's ultimate, inevitable connection in *The Music Man* (at least in a subtle way)—this time using a near partner song technique; the melody for Marian's longing ballad "Goodnight, My Someone" is basically the same melody used for "Seventy-Six Trombones" (both songs first heard in Act One). The obvious difference is that the former is a ballad; the latter is a march. Few audiences are ever aware of this clever twist of melodies that Meredith employed to, as he put it, "suggest that these two people possibly have more in common than meets the eye."[2] However, late in Act Two, Meredith gives these two a "double reprise" where they each reprise a line from these respective songs. Then in an ultimate "ah ha!" moment for Harold and the audience (Marian arrived there slightly earlier), they swap melodies with Harold singing a snippet of "Goodnight, My Someone" and Marian singing a bit of "Seventy-Six Trombones." Again, only the discerning audience ears in that moment may hear the similar melodies, but we now have clearly been shown through their melody swapping that our protagonist and antagonist hero and heroine are more alike than different, and more importantly, these two have finally found their romantic destiny.

You and I and the World

During Meredith's busy radio years, World War II was brewing and would inevitably draw in the United States. But before that happened, Meredith was still busy continuing to write songs throughout the decade. Songs such as "Iowa," "Two in Love," and "The Peony Bush" did well and were introduced on his various radio programs. But his first pop romantic song that really hit was "You and I." "You And I" reached number one on *Your Hit Parade* and sold a truckload of records for Meredith since Bing Crosby and Glenn Miller (among many others) recorded the song. The song eventually became the theme song for *Maxwell House Coffee Time*.

Because of some complications at the time among the music publishing world, Meredith self-published the song and obtained national distribution from Music Dealers Service of New York. When the song came back from the printer, the music ended on the next-to-last page leaving a blank page, so Meredith quickly penned another tune to fill that empty page on the reprint. Meredith scribbled a few "teaser" measures of music to promote another song just to fill the space he titled "Two in Love." After the second printing of "You and I," response was so strong for "Two in Love" that Meredith completed the song and released a separate piece of sheet music. "Two in Love" also then landed on *Your Hit Parade*!

Talk about a hot streak. But things were just heating up for Meredith.

"You And I" sheet music cover.
PHOTO COURTESY MEREDITH WILLSON PAPERS, GREAT
AMERICAN SONGBOOK FOUNDATION.

Lights, Cameras, Music

As World War II kept growing, legendary silent film star Charles Chaplin soon had Meredith and his music on his mind. And Hitler. Chaplin had heard and had been impressed with Meredith's second symphony, and accordingly he reached out to Meredith to score music for what would be Chaplin's first official talking picture.

The Great Dictator is a satirical comedy-drama film written, directed, produced, and starring Chaplin (costarring his then wife, Paulette Goddard). Even while Hollywood made the transition by and large to talking pictures, Chaplin continued to make silent films, eventually adding music to them to appease theatre owners in the talking picture era. By 1940, however, Chaplin saw the handwriting on the wall and knew it was time to cross the bridge to "the talkies." *The Great Dictator* was that.

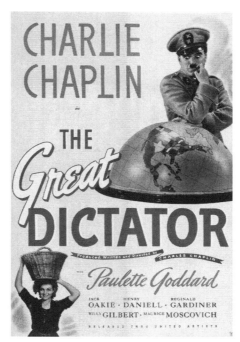

The Great Dictator *theatrical release poster.*
PUBLIC DOMAIN.

Chaplin's film advanced a stirring condemnation of Adolf Hitler, Benito Mussolini, fascism, antisemitism, and the Nazis. At the time of its release, the United States was still formally at peace with Nazi Germany and neutral during what were the early days of World War II. Still, when filming first began, Chaplin was warned by the studio that the film's subject matter was controversial and volatile, to say the least. Yet, Chaplin persisted, and the film was completed.

The Great Dictator was popular with audiences, becoming Chaplin's most commercially successful film ever, grossing $5 million, an impressive number in its time. Modern critics have praised it as a historically significant film and one of the greatest comedy films ever made, as well as an important work of satire. In 1997, it was selected by the Library of Congress for preservation in the U.S. National Film Registry as being "culturally, historically, or aesthetically significant."

Although Meredith did the "heavy lifting" on writing the music for the film, as usual, he gave credit where credit was due regarding Chaplin's influence on the score:

> I've seen [Chaplin] take a soundtrack and cut it all up and paste it back
> together and come up with some of the dangdest effects you ever heard—
> effects a composer would never think of. Don't kid yourself about that
> one. He would have been great at anything: music, law, ballet dancing, or
> painting—house, sign, or portrait. I got screen credit for *The Great Dicta-*
> *tor* music score, but the best parts of it were all Chaplin's ideas, like using
> [Wagner's] *Lohengrin* "Prelude" in the famous balloon-dance scene.[3]

According to Meredith, the scene in which Chaplin shaves a customer to
Brahms's *Hungarian Dance No 5* had been filmed before he arrived, using a
phonograph record for timing. Meredith's task was to rerecord it with a full
studio orchestra, fitting the music to the action. They had planned to do it
painstakingly, recording eight measures or less at a time, after running through
the entire scene to get the overall idea. Chaplin decided to record the run-
through in case anything was usable. Willson wrote:

> By dumb luck we had managed to catch every movement, and that was the
> first and only "take" made of the scene, the one used in the finished picture.[4]

Meredith's close collaboration with Chaplin during the production of the film
inevitably influenced some of his approach to comedic timing in his later creative efforts. "It was a real pleasure to watch him day after day and see him tick."[5]

The Great Dictator influenced numerous future directors, such as Stanley
Kubrick, Mel Brooks, Wes Anderson, and animator Chuck Jones. The film was
nominated for five Academy Awards, including one for Meredith's (and Chaplin's) score. In his 1964 autobiography, Chaplin stated that he could not have
made the film had he known about the true extent of the horrors of the Nazi
concentration camps at that time.

With his work on *The Great Dictator* completed, Meredith's phone rang
again to score another Hollywood film. This time, the gentleman caller was
none other than Sam Goldwyn. For thirty-five years in Hollywood, Goldwyn
had built a reputation in the motion picture business and developed an eye for
finding the talent for making successful films. William Wyler directed most of
his celebrated productions, hiring the hottest screenwriters of the day in Hollywood. For his next production, he had acquired screen rights to the recently

hit Broadway play *The Little Foxes*, by Lillian Hellman, who would also pen the film adaptation's screenplay. (The original Broadway production of the property starred Tallulah Bankhead in the lead role, with whom Meredith would work closely on a radio show in 1950.)

Meredith wrote about taking the assignment:

> Along about this time a fellow named Sam Goldwyn was producing a picture called *The Little Foxes*, and just because I didn't want to do the music for it he wanted me to, which is characteristic of Hollywood and Mr. Goldwyn. In fact, I guess, to some extent it's human nature. Anyhow, I got my gang together and we moved in on the Goldwyn Studio.[6]

The Little Foxes *theatrical release poster.*
PUBLIC DOMAIN.

And so, the work began. When the film was released, reviewer Bosley Crowther wrote in his review in the *New York Times*:

> Lillian Hellman's grim and malignant melodrama . . . has now been translated to the screen with all its original viciousness intact. . . . [It] leaps to the front as the most bitingly sinister picture of the year and as one of the most cruelly realistic character studies yet shown on the screen. Mr. Wyler, with the aid of [cinematographer] Gregg Toland, has used the camera to sweep in the myriad of small details of a mauve decadent household. . . . Miss [Bette] Davis's performance in the role which Tallulah Bankhead played so brassily on the stage is abundant with color and mood. *The Little Foxes* will not increase your admiration for mankind. But it is a very exciting picture to watch in a comfortably objective way, especially if you enjoy expert stabbing in the back.[7]

The film enjoyed excellent box office receipts, and Meredith was nominated the second time for an Academy Award (Best Scoring of a Dramatic Picture) for his work on the film. But Meredith's personal triumph with the film came in helping give the film's dark character lead her "comeuppance" at the end of the film.

> I had been arguing and arguing with Willie Wyler, the director, about the finish of the picture. It was none of my business, but the character played by Bette Davis had killed her husband, stolen from everybody, including her own brothers, and was so obnoxious that her own daughter finally told her off and left her flat—I'm just corny enough to want such a character to get her comeuppance and plenty, retribution and all like that.[8]

But the film ends with no punishment for Davis's character (Regina Giddens) at all, who goes on to live evidently happily ever after. When Meredith inquired about the ending to find out if Regina got her "just desserts," Wyler responded no, she didn't, and "nobody ever caught up with her and that's all there is to it." Meredith writes:

> Well, I hollered and screamed that there's always got to be Justice and she should at least look a little frightened or disturbed. In the last scene of the

picture, but Willie laughed at me and said, "Too late—the picture is shot—
it's done—it's over and finished. And I wouldn't change it even if I could,
which I wouldn't."[9]

Meredith had written a song for the film, "Never Feel Too Weary to Pray,"
which was cut in the film's final edit. But he was able to finagle a way to assert
his own subtle commentary into the film with his music for the closing credits
with that cut song. A chorus of voices sing these words just as the shot of Bette
Davis's face fades into "The End":

> O Lord, sound the trump of the Judgement,
> O Lord, hurry on to that day![10]

Meredith said that most people wouldn't notice that move, even if they stayed
to the end of the film, but his "Iowa conscience felt better."[11]

While scoring *The Little Foxes* and his radio work had absorbed much of
his time, Meredith managed to pen another classical piece, *The Jervis Bay*. This
twelve-minute "symphonic poem" as Meredith called it, was a tribute to World
War II soldiers fighting under terrible odds. Presented on a multinetwork
ninety-minute special *Greek War Relief Program*, writer Gene Fowler created
the spoken poem "The Jervis Bay Goes Down," which was dramatically read
(by British actor Ronald Colman over Meredith's music). The poem eloquently
depicts the sinking of an Australian freighter in the Atlantic Ocean during
wartime. The moving piece was well-received. One could say it was the calm
before the storm in the United States. As Meredith wrote:

> During our '40–'41 [radio] season benefits had become more and more
> frequent. Hardly a week went by without a special Red Cross broadcast or
> Bundles for Britain or Greek Relief or Russian Relief. And then one Sun-
> day morning, wham! We were at war, so everybody immediately began to
> worry about how he could best serve his country.[12]

Meredith would soon be trading his conducting baton and radio microphone in for an Army uniform, complete with a conducting baton and radio
microphone.

Seven

"TURN IT INTO A SHOW, MERE!"

Getting the idea for something . . . is the whole thing. Then you just sit down and write it.

—Meredith Willson

In 1949, the sun was starting to set on the so-called golden age of radio. The fledgling medium of television was still yet to hit its stride. And although Meredith had clearly enjoyed success on radio, finding steady and lucrative work on television had so far eluded him. Although the royalties on his hit song "May the Good Lord Bless and Keep You" were still helping "bless and keep" him and Rini, he was starting to get a "sinking feeling" regarding his career in radio and television. As he put it, he had "one foot on a departing boat, and the other on a receding dock."[1]

Then came a phone call that would eventually lead to the beginning of his next act. That call would start the ball rolling and would lead to Meredith's greatest career success. The call was from his good friend, Frank Loesser. But more on that later.

Long before his eventual Broadway successes, Loesser was known for the dozens of song hits from his days in Hollywood. He had supplied lyrics to the music of such greats as Jule Styne, Burton Lane, Hoagy Carmichael, and Arthur Schwartz, penning such songs as "I Don't Want to Walk Without You," "Two Sleepy People," "Heart and Soul," "They're Either Too Young or Too Old," and finally as composer/lyricist, "Spring Will Be a Little Late This Year," "On a Slow Boat to China," and his 1948 Academy Award winner, "Baby, It's Cold Outside."

In 1940, Loesser made his official composing debut with the music (and lyric) for the title song of the Paramount film *Seventeen*. World War II intervened, and PFC Frank Loesser was assigned to Armed Forces Radio Service (AFRS), providing lyrics for army camp shows. These so-called camp shows were daily entertainment shows performed by Hollywood stars in front of live audiences that were broadcast overseas. So the need for a lot of musical material was evident.

It was well-known in Hollywood circles that Meredith Willson was not only a successful and prolific songwriter but also fast and versatile. At parties where he and Rini attended (or hosted), he would inevitably be invited to a piano to casually entertain and would share many of his well-known and lesser-known songs. He could sit down at home and write a song on most any subject. (I saw that beautiful grand piano—with its matching, interlocking twin—on my visit with his widow, Rosemary, at their home in the Mandeville Canyon section of Brentwood, California, an LA suburb. She let me play a few notes on it, and I could almost feel the energy still emanating from the keys).

With the United States deeply involved in World War II, Uncle Sam—by way of the U.S. War Department—reached out to prolific hit songwriter Meredith. The War Department was interested in keeping morale and patriotism alive and well not only for the troops but also at home. They asked if Meredith would use his substantial songwriting skills to create music that would entertain and inspire for the war effort. Patriotic soul that he was, Meredith happily said yes.

His first assignment was for the home front in general, and truck drivers in specific. After all, truck drivers were keeping the economy (and often war supplies) moving. The result was a song composed by Meredith in a matter of hours titled "My Ten-Ton Baby and Me." It soon appeared in a trucker's magazine. And that was it. Soon forgotten.

What followed over the weeks and months to come were more assignments from the War Department for Meredith. The result was a string of songs that were for different military divisions and needs: "Gangway, You Rats, Gangway" (for the USO); "Yankee Doodle Girl" (Women's Air Corps); "Hit the Leather" (Cavalry); and "Fire Up, Carry On to Victory!" (Chemical Warfare). Some of the songs were never used, but in typical Meredith fashion, he was undaunted.

His patriotic solution: He enlisted in the Army and was promptly (and naturally) assigned to AFRS. But he did not have to serve overseas. The powers-that-were in the military naturally knew his talents were best used at home and on radio. Therefore, as with Loesser, Meredith shared an association with AFRS.

Meredith's career with AFRS took off, and by 1944, he was involved with providing music or musical direction for more than one hundred programs weekly, including shows such as *GI Journal, Front Line Theater, Jubilee, Mail Call,* and *At Ease* to name several. His finest moments with AFRS were probably with the successful show *Command Performance,* which featured top Hollywood stars of the day, such as Bing Crosby, Judy Garland, Frank Sinatra, Errol Flynn, and the Andrews Sisters. As became his niche in radio, Meredith served as the musical director and conductor of the show. The first *Command Performance* was broadcast on March 1, 1942, almost exactly three months after the bombing of Pearl Harbor. It was produced under the aegis of the U.S. Office of War Information, and its big success actually paved the way for the creation of AFRS in May 1942.

Command Performance aired from 1942 to 1949. Most episodes were produced before an audience in the Vine Street Playhouse in Hollywood and recorded via electrical transcriptions (ETs, special phonograph recordings made exclusively for radio broadcasting during its golden age). These ETs were transmitted by shortwave to the troops overseas and not broadcast over domestic U.S. radio stations. The 1942 Christmas Eve performance of the program was the only program of the series to be broadcast to a general U.S. audience. Troops sent in requests for a particular performer to appear, and they also suggested unusual ideas for music, sketches, or sounds on the program. For example, they fulfilled requests for dancer Ann Miller tap-dancing in military boots or Bing Crosby mixing a drink for Bob Hope. The announcer's weekly proclamation at the beginning of the show to all the troops listening and to whose troops' requests were chosen was, "Buddy, your request is our command!" *Time* magazine described *Command Performance* as "the best wartime program in America."

By 1949, Meredith had wrapped up his three successful years of patriotic duties with AFRS when fellow AFRS alum Loesser made what would be that pivotal phone call to him, planting the first seeds of a possible new direction in Meredith's career. And like all servicemen who had concluded their service, Meredith needed to restart his interrupted civilian career.

Destiny Calls

Frank said simply to Meredith on the phone call, "I think you ought to write a musical comedy about Iowa."

And Meredith simply said to Frank, "No."

"I thought it was a good idea," Meredith later recalled years later, "and I wanted very much to do it. But I refused, just to prove Frank was wrong."[2]

Talk about Iowa stubborn.

Despite what would eventually become the handwriting on the wall of the music business and his place in it, Meredith was being prudent and cautious with his career. You couldn't blame him. The waters of musical comedy were (and are) extremely hazardous. Meredith didn't think such a risky venture was worth his time and creative energy, at least at that point in his career.

It was no wonder that Loesser had Broadway on his mind for his friend Meredith. In 1948, theatrical producers Cy Feuer and Ernie Martin lured him back East from his work in Hollywood to create a score for their musical version of *Charley's Aunt. Where's Charley?* became Frank's first hit show, and with a score that included "Once in Love with Amy" and "Make a Miracle," it proved that Frank was more than just a writer of pop tunes from Hollywood—not that there's anything wrong with that!

Now it could be Meredith's turn to prove he, too, was more than a writer of pop tunes and a music director. Not that he had anything to prove, necessarily. He had certainly enjoyed a successful career up to that point. But again, the entertainment worlds of radio and television were changing during that period of his life, and he had to be aware and adapt, or become extinct.

Some exciting new opportunities appeared for Meredith in 1950, first in the form of an invitation to write a new fight song for the University of Iowa. In October of that year, Cedar Rapids *Gazette* music columnist Les Zachels opined that he thought the old fight song was outdated. A new song was needed, he wrote, and Meredith Willson was just the person to pen it (even though Meredith didn't attend nor graduate from the institution). Other editorial writers echoed Zachels's thoughts, and the idea gained momentum. So Zachels sent the collective clippings to Meredith at his California home. Always one to answer the call from his home folk, Meredith quickly turned out a tune that captured hearts immediately when it was premiered on his national radio program on New Year's Eve 1950. It was officially premiered in Iowa at an Iowa-Indiana basketball game on February 12, 1951, during the half-time break. When an interviewer asked Meredith how the tune came so easily and quickly, he said simply, "Getting the idea for something like that is the whole thing. Then you just sit down and write it."

Also in 1950, Meredith couldn't help but notice (along with countless others) his friend Frank's next Broadway effort, *Guys and Dolls*, which opened to rave reviews in November, winning the Tony Award for Best Musical. Frank's score was lush with hits, including "A Bushel and a Peck," "Luck Be a Lady," and "Sit Down, You're Rocking the Boat." The show eventually became one of the most enduring classics of the American musical theatre. But then, it was "just" a solid current hit but clearly enough to resonate with Meredith. This also wasn't lost on Meredith's friend Goodman Ace. "Goody" (as he was known to his friends) was not always the most recognizable writer/performer of his era by today's reader or listener, but his low-key, literate, and droll approach to writing and performing made him one of the most sought-after writers in radio and television from the 1930s through the 1960s.

While *Guys and Dolls* was lighting up the Broadway stage, *The Big Show* (as discussed in chapter 2) premiered the same month Sunday evenings on NBC. As noted previously, Meredith had landed the job of the musical director for this big-budget, last-gasp radio effort, starring the always unpredictable Tallulah Bankhead. Goody was the head writer on the show, and he joined Loesser in his exhortation for Meredith to write a musical comedy based on his Iowan roots in Mason City. After all, Meredith often used the on-air repartee he had with "Miss Bankhead, sir" (as he called Tallulah Bankhead, the show's star, due to her smoky, deep voice) to promote his beloved hometown of Mason City, all to Tallulah's hilarious chagrin.

"You should turn these funny stories you tell Tallulah on air about your hometown into a musical," Goody told Meredith.

And Meredith, still Iowa-stubborn to the core replied, "No . . . I can't do it. As much as I would like to try."[3] Meredith was committed still to radio and yes, that new thing called television.

Bring on the Books

Unfortunately, *The Big Show* was in some ways a big disappointment. It was cancelled after only two seasons. Although ratings had been respectable over-all, television's inroads continued to erode radio's power and finances. Plus, with *The Big Show*'s large budget of $100,000 per episode, it made profitability much tougher. And it was becoming increasingly difficult for radio to compete with the novelty of television (weak as its early offerings were in comparison to established radio shows). Therefore, in large market cities, precious advertising dollars were being siphoned from radio to the exciting and promising new medium of television. But even with the demise of *The Big Show*, NBC, like all radio networks of the day that were jumping onto the television bandwagon, transposed what worked in their successful radio shows onto their new tele-vision shows. Accordingly, a shorter (and smaller budget version) of *The Big Show* soon aired on NBC-TV. Retitled *Four-Star Revue*, it boasted a weekly budget of $50,000 (second at the time only to NBC's *Colgate Comedy Hour*). The series originally starred four celebrities: Ed Wynn, Danny Thomas, Jack Carson, and Jimmy Durante (hence the name *Four Star Revue*). These celeb-rities alternated as hosts of the program each week. Beginning in its second season, additional stars would join the show, causing the title to change to *All Star Revue*. By the show's third season, Tallulah Bankhead and Meredith Will-son re-created their former *Big Show* radio roles for *All Star Revue* on a rotating basis with the other hosts. It was *Big Show* déjà vu when Tallulah opened with a monologue followed by sketches and songs, with Meredith at the conducting podium. Her opening line was "Welcome to Tallulahvision!" followed by a new song Meredith had written titled "Hallelujah, It's Tallulahvision at Last." The show also boasted the Ron Fletcher Dancers and stars such as Groucho Marx, Ethel Barrymore, Bert Lahr, and Fred MacMurray. Another *Big Show* moment happened in the Tallulah/Meredith iteration of the show when the cast closed with Meredith's hit "May the Good Lord Bless and Keep You."[4]

Despite placing a respectable twentieth in the 1952–1953 television season, *All Star Revue* was cancelled at the end of the season.

I was president of music publisher Shawnee Press, Inc., for four years (2005–2009). Shawnee Press was founded by bandleader and choral conducting legend Fred Waring (of Fred Waring and the Pennsylvanians fame). When I became president of Shawnee, Fred had been deceased for more than twenty years. But I became good friends with his widow, Virginia. Fred and Virginia were close to Meredith and Rini Willson. Virginia and I spoke about Meredith and Fred on many occasions and why neither of them enjoyed tremendous success on television.

"Fred didn't like the discipline that television took compared to the easier format that radio afforded," Virginia said. "Had Fred liked television more or Meredith had gotten a big break in television, I believe either one of them could have given Lawrence Welk a run for his money."[5] Although, it is known that Welk, Waring, and Meredith were good friends, so if any rivalry ever existed, it did so beneath the surface. But there was no evidence whatsoever of any such competition among them.

Meredith's career in broadcasting certainly didn't end with the cancellation of *The Big Show* and *All Star Revue*. Also, during the 1952–1953 season, he channeled his classical music roots and joined opera singers Robert Merrill and Margaret Piazza for a thirty-minute Monday night program of serious music titled *Encore*, also on NBC. In addition to *Encore*, he also appeared on several other radio shows: *Every Day* was a fifteen-minute weekday program with Meredith noodling at the piano, cohosted by Rini. This show ran through 1954 and featured editorials from newspapers across the country, with Meredith and Rini adding their own brand of fun comments. When *Every Day* ran its course, *Weekday*, a show similarly formatted with a few tweaks to freshen things up, aired with Meredith and Rini from 1955 to 1956. Also, the aforementioned *Meredith Willson's Music Room* continued through the 1951–1952 season.

Still, with an eye on the fledgling medium of television, to keep things moving ahead in his career, he reduced his involvement in radio so as to attempt to break into television once and for all. But as previously documented, his television work was spotty and ultimately didn't add up to setting the stage for the next big thing. Perhaps writing books would be the next chapter.

Meredith had tried his hand at being a book author, and after a few false starts, the first published result was a successful book titled *And There I Stood with My Piccolo*. Originally released in 1948, it was a zesty and colorful memoir of Meredith's early years—from growing up in Iowa, to playing the flute with John Philip Sousa's band and the New York Philharmonic Orchestra, to his successful career in composing for radio and film in Hollywood. It was apparent to everyone, except maybe Meredith himself, that he was on his way to something big. Although Meredith loved the title of his new book, he had second thoughts about it when, at a public signing of the new book, he was approached by a woman who said she was delighted for him to sign his new book, *Is My Piccolo Showing?*[6]

Several years passed before he was able to tackle a second book. Published in 1952, his next book was not a memoir, but a novel titled *Who Did What to Fedalia?* This was Meredith's only foray into fiction for the book world. The novel follows Iowan Fedalia Parker and her dream of being a professional singer after enjoying success on the autoharp. Although the comic work was a miss in many ways, it gave Meredith his first try at story structure and developing characters.

In 1955, his next memoir was released, *Eggs I Have Laid*. Back in familiar territory of sharing folksy stories of his career, it was a success, due to his down-home Iowa tone as he waxed humorously and philosophically about Mason City, John Phillip Sousa, his career in the radio business, and life at home with Rini. But authoring another book, successful as it was, still hadn't provided him with the next big career step he needed.

Enter Feuer and Martin, Center Stage

As 1955 rolled over to 1956, Meredith's fears had become reality: His appearances as a star on major radio programs had dried up because, for the most part, those radio variety shows had completely dried up. Also, by now, a certain young man named Elvis Presley had made his first recordings for RCA, and the winds of change in the music business were starting to blow, which would greatly impact radio, the medium that had been Meredith's bread and butter for decades. Fortunately, however, rewinding to 1951, he had finally relinquished his Iowa-stubborn status about tackling a musical comedy.

It was Cy Feuer and Ernest ("Ernie") Martin, with Frank Loesser whispering in their ears, who approached Meredith in 1951 about—yes—writing a musical comedy about growing up in Mason City. Frank wasn't about to give up on his belief that Meredith had what it took to write a show. And Feuer and Martin were the hottest producing team on Broadway at the time, with Frank's *Guys and Dolls* enjoying a hit Broadway run, which they produced.

I had the honor of visiting with Feuer in his Manhattan penthouse when he was ninety-one years young (I say young because Feuer was truly seemingly as sharp as ever at that age, and his memory was replete with great stories about Meredith and Rini he shared with me, which I have included in this book). Details later.

Feuer was a theater producer, director, composer, musician, and half of the legendary producing duo Feuer and Martin. He was the winner of three Tony Awards plus a lifetime achievement Tony.

Born Seymour Arnold Feuerman in Brooklyn, he became a professional trumpet player at the age of fifteen, working at clubs on weekends to help support his family while attending high school. It was there he first met Abe Burrows, who in later years he would hire to write the book for *Guys and Dolls*. Having no interest in mathematics, science, or sports, he dropped out of school and found work as a trumpet player on a political campaign truck. He later studied at the Juilliard School before joining the orchestras at the Roxy Theater and later Radio City Music Hall. In 1938, he toured the country with Leon Belasco and his orchestra, eventually ending up in Burbank, California, where he also decided to study film scoring.

In 1947, having decided he had no real talent for film scoring (even though he'd received five Oscar nominations), Feuer returned to New York City, where he teamed up with Ernie Martin, who had been the head of comedy programming at CBS Radio. After an aborted attempt to stage a production based on George Gershwin's *An American in Paris*, they produced *Where's Charley?* Although six of the seven major New York critics panned it, positive word of mouth about the show, particularly Ray Bolger's star turn in it, kept it running for three years. Over the next several decades, Feuer and Martin mounted some of the most notable titles in the Broadway musical canon, including the aforementioned *Guys and Dolls,* then *How to Succeed in Business Without Really Trying*, both of which won the Tony Award for Best Musical. As of this writing, *How to Succeed in Business Without Really Trying* is one of only seven musicals to have won the Pulitzer Prize for Drama.

Feuer was also a stage director. Among his Broadway directing credits were *Little Me* and the ill-fated *I Remember Mama*. Feuer's greatest career success was the 1972 film version of *Cabaret*, which won eight Academy Awards, winning him a Best Picture Oscar nomination as the film's credited producer. (*Cabaret* lost Best Picture to *The Godfather*, but Feuer won a Golden Globe for Best Motion Picture, Musical or Comedy.) With Martin, they were responsible for the 1985 screen adaptation of *A Chorus Line*, which proved to be one of their biggest flops. In addition to producing, Feuer served as president, and later chairman, of the League of American Theatres and Producers (now called The Broadway League) from 1989 to 2003.

In Meredith's book *But He Doesn't Know the Territory*, Meredith describes his first exchange with Feuer and Martin sharing their idea with him about writing a show:

> They said, "Mere, we think you could write a musical comedy."
>
> And I say, "What about?"
>
> And they says, "About your Iowa boyhood, with the common touch you have occasionally demonstrated as in this song you recently wrote for Tallulah's radio program 'May the Good Lord Bless and Keep You.'"
>
> Ernie says, "You also had the common touch in your book a few years back. Something about *There You Stood with Your Piccolo*."
>
> "'*And There I Stood with My Piccolo*,'" I says, surprised and flattered but trying not to sound it. "I'll have to think about it."[7]

Meredith adds, "Actually, Rini had suggested I write a musical comedy 6,741 times before, pointing out that along with the music I had written a lot of lyrics through the years and a couple of books—why shouldn't I combine forces with myself in a musical comedy?" He goes on to say:

So, one day, without giving the matter too much thought, I wrote ACT
ONE, SCENE ONE on the empty paper, not, of course, to show these people that I could write a musical comedy but to show them I could not. And
for the next six years I was way out in front.[8]

"Act One, Scene One." So far so good, said Meredith. "It's the fifth word that
was the sticker. Couldn't locate that fifth word. So I just sat there. Quite some
time went by. Three years, in fact."[9]

Meredith did get up from his typewriter during those three years, he hastened to add. Meredith was proving himself wrong this time, when he'd said
(regarding the Iowa Fight Song), "Getting the idea for something like that is
the whole thing. Then you just sit down and write it." Well, he'd sat down to
write this new musical comedy about his Iowa boyhood. He just couldn't seem
to write it. Or perhaps he was continuing to succeed in proving Feuer and
Martin and Loesser were wrong.

To break his writer's block, to get "oiled up" (as Meredith put it) and past
the words "Act One, Scene One," Meredith started writing what he called his
"priming essays." He wrote about several childhood memories, his years in the
Sousa band, you name it. Anything to "sneak up" on that typewriter and get the
next words out. But still, nothing came.

"Well, ya got trouble, my friend."

With a capital "T" and that rhymes with "G" and that stands for "Get me
out of here. . . . what am I doing trying to write a musical comedy?"

Eight

FATE AND FEUER AND MARTIN

When we heard Meredith's first draft of his show, Ernie and I believed it could be a hit.

—Cy Feuer

Long before Feuer and Martin approached Meredith with the idea of writing a musical comedy, the medium of television had been growing steadily. That medium would have an impact on Meredith's pursuit of writing *The Music Man.*

Electronic television was first successfully demonstrated in San Francisco in 1927. By 1946, the number of U.S. homes with television sets in use was approximately six thousand. Five short years later in 1951, the number of sets in use had mushroomed to some twelve million. No new invention had entered U.S. homes faster than black-and-white television sets. By 1955, half of all U.S. homes had one set; by the late 1990s, 98 percent of U.S. homes had at least one television set, and those sets were on for an average of more than seven hours a day. So in 1951 with the growth and popularity of television starting to eclipse radio (heretofore Meredith's bread-and-butter medium), Meredith had his antenna up for opportunities in television when Feuer and Martin were pitching Meredith on the idea of writing a show. And that he couldn't seem to get past writing more than the first four words ("Act One, Scene One") of this new musical play he was trying to write, a potential solid and lucrative gig on this burgeoning new medium seemed irresistible. Meredith said he "had to keep the store open, which gave me considerable pause, what with my old profession in radio . . . dwindling away from me and my new profession as playwright refusing to progress beyond the first four words." He therefore "had one foot in a departing boat and the other on a receding dock."[1]

And then the phone rang. Again.

This time, it wasn't Feuer and Martin (they had planted their musical comedy idea seeds with Meredith, hoping they would take root while they moved on to another successful project). No, the good news phone call came from Meredith's "agent's agent." He told Meredith he had received an offer to fly immediately to New York to audition for a new TV quiz show (television pilot) called *The Big Surprise* involving a $100,000 jackpot question, especially big money in those days. Meredith was told he was practically all set to be the emcee. The producer of the show was also producer of the big TV hit, *$64,000 Question*. This was too attractive to turn down.

Meredith immediately and easily laid aside his playwriting work. He and Rini were on the next available plane to New York from Los Angeles and arrived the next day. His agent met them with more good news.

"They're pretty happy with you in the emcee spot, Meredith," said the agent. "Your Iowa style will be real offbeat, they think. In fact for the audition, they are doing a complete performance in NBC's Studio 6B with sponsor, agency, contestants, camera, and *audience*. That's how *sure* they are."[2]

(In NBC's New York Rockefeller Center broadcast facilities, each of the studios are laden with rich broadcast history. Studio 6B, as of this writing, is the current home of NBC's *Tonight Show Starring Jimmy Fallon*.)

Meredith was flying high from his agent's encouraging words when he walked into the first production meeting of the highly anticipated bigger-than-that-$64,000 question show. As he spoke to the show's producer in their first meeting, he mused and strategized on how he could find places in a tightly timed game show for moments to ad-lib his "Iowa style." The producer quickly interrupted: "No, no, Meredith, just say, 'You're *right!* You're absolutely *right!*' And, Meredith"—he took a confidential tone—"throw yourself forward on the ball of your foot as you say it." Meredith replied, "You're *right!* You're *absolutely right!*" "Fine," said the producer.

"*Right*, you're *absolutely right!*" Meredith repeated for clarity. "Do you want me to always say that?"

"Oh yes," replied the producer. "Oh yes. Sounds good."

"Right," said Meredith.[3]

He was given a dummy script of the show to study before the big audition pilot, complete with cameras and glittering scenery. And when showtime arrived the next day, according to Meredith:

> The show opened with shadow effects and electronic music and echo-chamber voices. First, a private detective was introduced, psychologically making everything safe and expensive and official. Then an IBM machine, making everything modern and honest. Then I came springing out. Ever see people come springing out? That's a trick you accomplish merely by walking back a few steps into the wings as you hear your cue, then when you come forward again you have a couple extra yards in which to gain momentum before you're visible and you come out onto the gol-darn stage like you were shot out of a bow. So I shot myself on stage, right up to an elaborate space-age podium—chrome and shining—almost over-shot it, in fact. And in a very few moments I was crying out "You're *right!* You're *absolutely right!*" to the first contestant, leaning into my delivery as instructed. I cried out like this to two more contestants, even once for a wrong answer. And then. And then. This lady came up, see, and got her winnings up to $50,000. The $100,000 question was next. It danced on the top half of my card in front of my eyes. The answer to the question was on the bottom half. A very dramatic silence closed in. Leaning forward onto the ball of my right foot, and summoning my loudest clearest tones, I read the lady the *answer* instead of the *question.*[4]

Meredith added, "I think the company got out of it without paying her the full $100,000 but I never found out for sure."[5]

Rini took all of this in from the audience. When the program finished, and she went up to Meredith, he took her arm and she said quietly, "Very nice, dear." Calmly looking around, they went across the stage, out into the back, smiling at those whom they encountered as they made a graceful, yet hasty exit . . . down the steps, past the control room, down the elevator to the lobby, and into the Manhattan street. As Meredith and Rini exited the studio, they got the complete cold shoulder from everyone involved with the show—the director, the advertising agency executives, the sponsors, even the audience members.

"Nor the elevator man. Not even my agent. In fact, we never heard from any of those people again," wrote Meredith.[6]

Meredith said he and Rini were "thoughtfully desperate" about the whole thing back in their hotel room that night. Nor did they rest well. Accordingly they slept in—past lunch. About four o'clock in the afternoon that next day, they called for room service for some food.

> Suddenly we burst out laughing. *And* we screamed. *And* we hollered. *And* we roared. *And* we got back on the plane and went home to California. For a while we just sat around screaming, "You're *right*. You're *absolutely right*" at each other.[7]

Meredith showed once again he could lay a substantial egg and laugh about it. But with a television pilot flop under his belt, and the diminished medium of radio gnawing at him, he was motivated now more than ever to dig into the musical play.

The Play's the Thing

Prior to his and Rini's New York game show audition trip, as referenced in the previous chapter, Meredith would write what he called his "priming essays" to "prime the [writing] pump" as it were. "I remembered that the composer Von Weber was a dead-center man who couldn't compose for sour apples until he first hit a D and an F-sharp on the piano," wrote Meredith. "He'd listen to those vibrations for a while and all of a sudden, he was a ball of fire. I tried D and F-sharp on the piano myself. Nothing."[8]

So instead of relying on random notes on the piano, he continued rattling off his priming essays. For example:

> I glanced absently up at a picture of some guys I have framed up over the desk there in my music room. Being nearsighted I was only able to pick out the one blond kid . . . what the heck was his name again? All of a sudden, I was typing. Tank, I wrote. Alvin Tank. He was the oldest. He's holding an alto [horn]. It is a picture of Mason City's first High School Band, back in 1912. One piccolo (me), two clarinets, two cornets, one euphonium, one

tuba, one snare drum, one bass drum, one trombone and Alvin Tank with this alto. We are all grimly posed in the non-smiling tradition of group picture-taking of those days. Alvin and Mama used to visit out in front of the house whenever Alvin passed by. Also Kilroy. Kilroy was another friend of Mama's. Any kid who passed the house was Mama's friend—there was no Catholic, no Protestant, no Jew to Mama, no black, white, tan, red, yellow, no big, little, rich, or poor. They were all just Middle-West kids to Mama, who, Mama always said, ought to be exposed to a little gentleness and gentility—a couple of good thoughts, and a few nice things, a book, a picture, a quotation, a poem. And the dang kids listened to her, too, even though her advice was not only about what to read but how to act—things kids don't usually like from adults. Got to get Mama into this show.[9]

And get Mama into the show he did. In several ways. Case in point: the lyrics to Marian the Librarian's soaring "I want" ballad clearly echo how Meredith lovingly described his Mama. The song, "My White Knight," occurs near the end of Act One:

> My white knight, not a Lancelot, nor an angel with wings.
> Just someone to love me, who is not ashamed of a few nice things.
> And if occasionally he'd ponder,
> What makes Shakespeare and Beethoven great,
> Him I could love 'til I die.[10]

More writing fleshed out Kilroy:

Kilroy seemed older than even the older kids, but I don't think he was, as I look back. He was smaller than any of the older kids. I think he only seemed older because he didn't go to school. He worked. I only know I was scared of him playing football the way he came tearing down the school yard packing that ball, hollering about his twenty-six operations. [We would all say at the beginning of the game]: "Come on Kilroy! Kilroy's gotta be on our side" And Kilroy would throw off his coat and charge in there—already sputtering about his operations in his high-pitched voice. "I had twenty-six operations! And I can still run you guys ragged!" He always seemed to be running sideways even though he was coming straight at you. I've thought about Kilroy before; a good many times through the years. Quite a good many times. I bet all the guys have. I know I have.[11]

These essays, centered around those childhood memories of Mason City, would get him moving creatively (he hoped) so he could fill that intimidating first blank page up with something. *Anything.* He had also written twenty (!) songs about those people and the situations therein. He asked himself, "Should I try to peddle this stuff individually? Forget trying to write in play form? Should I? Or shouldn't I?"[12]

But despite those essays and songs, Blank Page number one of this show-to-be still loomed like a cloud over him. Meredith again relied on his priming essays for inspiration, along with the songs he had written for the piece thus far. "In a quiet rage I continued on, with description at the edge and dialogue in the middle, dividing the material as seemed logical into three acts and seventeen scenes."[13] Soon, he had located "word number five."

Finally . . . the essays and songs had paid off. Meredith's "quiet rage" had propelled him. Alvin and Kilroy (along with his mama and many other Mason City citizens and memories—and especially that picture of the Mason City boys' band) had paved the way for his first start. He had finally broken through that often-toughest part of writing a major work (or any work): Filling in the first page . . . and completing a first draft of this show he called *The Silver Triangle.*

The story was about a boys' band. It starred a phony band leader and instrument salesman by the name of Harold Hill, actually a con man. As near as I could judge it ran about three hours and forty-five minutes which was pretty near two hours longer than necessary. Or desirable. Meanwhile, since I had last seen Feuer and Martin they had followed their famous production of *Guys and Dolls* with *Can Can*, another big hit, and were already starting on two more: *The Boy Friend* for September and *Silk Stockings* for Christmas. On the theory that if you want something done contact a busy man, I wired them: *Have combination essay, dialogue and song.* That same day Feuer and Martin answered: *Bring it to New York immediately.*[14]

Two nights later, Meredith and Rini were at Cy Feuer's house in New York ready to perform all the parts and sing all the songs. Of course, they had high hopes that Feuer and Martin, the hottest producers on Broadway at that time, would respond positively.

At Home with Cy

As referenced in the previous chapter, I had the honor and pleasure of getting to visit with Cy Feuer at that home many years later. By now in his career, he was often called by his peers and others "The Last Great Broadway Showman."

Feuer was dressed in a smart blue blazer and slacks, crisp shirt, and ascot. He led me to their beautiful living room, replete with Broadway memorabilia, awards, and the like. We sat, and his wife, Posy, joined us and also greeted me cordially.

Here was a man of elegance and style, even at the age of ninety-one. His wit and mind were seemingly as sharp as ever.

"Make yourself comfortable, Mark," he said as he offered me something to drink. His Brooklyn accent was not erased after years of being a world traveler.

"It's an honor to meet you and Mrs. Feuer," I said.

"Please call me Cy," he replied.

After settling in, I got right to it.

"I would love to talk about a lot of things this afternoon," I started, "but I can't resist starting with your late, great friends Meredith and Rini Willson." Without missing a beat, Cy laughs and says, "They ate birdseed." "I beg your pardon," I reply. Still smiling, Cy hastens to add, "Oh, not actual birdseed . . . but a lot of health food. Grains and seeds and things to keep them in tip-top shape. In addition to other regular food." "It must have worked," I say, "Since they certainly remained productive well into their upper years." He agreed. And then I asked him about the story that, according to Meredith Willson in his book *But He Doesn't Know the Territory*, he credited Cy and Ernie with coming up with the name of his immortal show.

"That's right. Meredith wanted to call the show *The Silver Triangle*, but Ernie and I weren't crazy about that title. We told Mere that he needed a million-dollar name for his show, and *The Silver Triangle* was not it."

Cy continued: "Mere's original subplot involved a disabled child with cerebral palsy in a wheelchair. Meredith believed strongly in telling the story that these children were misunderstood and underestimated. He wanted people to know these children's physical disability does not limit them mentally."[15] But rewinding back to that very first hearing of the show's first draft by Feuer and Martin, just what did they think?

According to Meredith, Feuer and Martin didn't just speak but "sprayed words" and spoke "a mile a minute, and always in short, alternating bursts."[16]

> C: "The score is great."
>
> E: "Of course we gotta change the title."
>
> C: "*The Silver Triangle* sounds like an Ibsen satire. About somebody's middle-aged mistress. At the Cherry Lane. Need a real Broadway title for a musical. You know a Broadway title when you hear it. And that it ain't. And you've gotta watch the disabled boy."
>
> E: "He's news, wonderful news, but he'll steal every scene."
>
> C: "Main thing is to prune him down. And shift the accent to the love story. Harold Hill is great. Larcenous guys like that are always great. Sky Masterson. What's-his-name Ravenal [from *Show Boat*]. And what a racket. Band instruments yet!"[17]

Of course, Meredith and Rini "floated home to the hotel in the early morning with our grinnings and head-shakings. We went to bed but not to sleep." "My gosh!" Rini said suddenly sitting up in the dark. "If they'd liked you on that $100,000 thing, you would never have written *The Silver Triangle*!" "You're *right! You're absolutely right!*" Meredith replied. Showing his true naiveté as a Broadway novice at this point, Meredith then said to Rini, "all except for a little pruning and shifting . . . and a new title, it's *done*." He added, "Wonder what we ought to call it?" And then they finally went to sleep.[18] They headed back home to California the next morning.

Two weeks after that auspicious night of Meredith's new show presentation, Cy and Ernie phoned Meredith from the Beverly Hills Hotel. Ernie opened, with Cy on the extension.[19]

E: "Josh Logan was very interested. Tied up for a year, though."

C: "With the Picnic movie. And a thing called *Bus Stop*."

E: "Also we got a title."

C: "Like to try it out on you."

E: "Are you sitting down?"

M: "Go ahead, I'm sitting down."

C: "Not over the phone, Ernie. We'll be right over."[20]

Cy then described to me the moment he and Ernie shared their title for Meredith's new show:

> When we drove up in their driveway, as they came out of the door to greet us, I didn't say hello or anything. . . . I just shouted out, "*The Music Man.* That's your title, Mere." And Mere immediately said, "I like it fine." Then he looked at Rini, who said, "Me too." And that was that.[21]

So now Meredith had that "million-dollar" Broadway title for his show. And the show just needed some tweaks and pruning. Certainly opening night couldn't be too far away!

Unbeknownst to Meredith and Rini at this point, that opening night was still several years away. And between that million-dollar title Feuer and Martin had given him and opening night were *thirty-eight rewrites* and numerous songs written only to be tossed out. Meredith was about to experience a new definition of endurance and perseverance.

Nine

THE BEST AND WORST OF TIMES

Words holler at me.

—Meredith Willson

Meredith's writing of the book for *The Music Man* had often centered on pleasing Ernie Martin up to this point in the story. After all, Martin was a writer himself with hit Broadway production credentials. But when he and Martin hit what seemed to be a creative brick wall regarding structural considerations for the show, Meredith saw Cy Feuer and Martin's original enthusiasm for the show start to wane, and that the producing duo moved on to focus on other projects didn't help Meredith's creative state of mind. With Meredith scrambling to keep cash flowing for a livelihood, he and Rini attempted to step up their personal appearances for local music groups and colleges. Those appearances had been a consistent needed revenue stream for them during those days. And just when he felt as if *The Music Man* might have to be shelved permanently, Meredith's phone rang in his Brentwood home on a fall afternoon in 1955. And the last person (or persons) from whom he would have expected to hear was an excited Feuer and Martin on the other end. Feuer described the call to me:

> Meredith had continued to tinker with his musical but Ernie and I had moved on with other projects. But we hadn't forgotten his show. We had a good relationship with [CBS-TV chairman] Bill Paley and [CBS-TV president] Frank Stanton. We were in a meeting with them discussing several projects, and Ernie brought up *The Music Man*. We told them all about the concept, Meredith's passion for the show, and how we thought it had

excellent potential. If CBS would invest $100,000 to produce a television version of the show, that would mean their network would be the first to present an original Broadway musical comedy. They agreed on the spot and offered a full two hours of network airtime devoted to the show—to be broadcast on a Sunday night, pre-empting the hit *Ed Sullivan Show*! Such a thing was unheard of back then. We called Meredith to fill him in on the proposal, and he was naturally over the moon about it.[1]

Indeed, Meredith was thrilled at the prospect of a major television network shelling out $100,000 to launch his musical through an historic telecast, which included a sizeable advance and potential royalties for Meredith. Such cash was an opportunity he certainly couldn't turn down. But his excitement was, once again, doused within a week's time. Meredith was at the NBC Studios recording another installment of his *How to Listen to Longhair Music* radio program when he was summoned for an important long-distance telephone call. Feuer and Martin were once again on the other end, "spraying" words at him.

"Deal's off," Feuer said. "Couldn't agree on the casting with the agency. We told the agency, 'Who needs your okay on casting? Either we're the producers or we aren't.'" Martin chimed in, "They called back this morning okaying everything, but we said 'Too late.' Three weeks later they'd be trying to run something else, so we pulled out. Sorry, Mere. Be talkin' to you."[2]

And that was it. Just as fast as a possible big deal for the show had been done, it was undone.

Then, it was November . . . then, December 1955. Meredith continued to ponder his show with its talking-rhymeless-rhythm songs as his way to bridge dialogue and song. In January of the next year, Meredith received a small newspaper clipping from the *New York Times* somebody sent him that read: *Feuer & Martin have tabled* The Music Man *in order to concentrate on other plans.*

So now it was official. No more Feuer and Martin to champion *The Music Man*. And Meredith was once again left alone at his typewriter, the latest draft of his show (which still needed a lot of rewrites) and no real prospects to produce it. Meredith described how things continued to plod along:

> February was usually a good month for me. I spent it badly the year of '56, however, trying to get a draft together that would accommodate the new

stuff I liked and still pare down some of the awful overlength. At the end of
the month I had a new draft and it wasn't any two hours too long either—it
was two hours and a half too long.[3]

One of the main sticklers was still the disabled child. Said Meredith, "When
you have a twelve-year-old character with a brilliant mind locked up in a body
with no muscular control to where everyone takes for granted he's crazy, as
people did in 1912 (and still do, far too many of them), you have an awful
time keeping such a boy from not only stealing his scenes, but from stealing
the entire show."[4] Meredith stated he even tried one draft where the audience
never saw the child onstage at all. The love story, meanwhile, between Harold
and Marian was getting stronger and stronger, "but you'd never notice it with
that wheelchair kid in the show,"[5] added Meredith.

But he remained steadfast. Then one day, Meredith heard from Jesse Lasky,
a Hollywood film producer of legendary status. Lasky had been at a party a
week before, along with other Tinseltown luminaries, where Meredith and
Rini casually played several songs and recited some dialogue from the show.
Meredith was often urged to the piano at parties, where he would gregariously
and easily hold those gathered 'round in the palm of his hand, as Rini would
sing. So it was natural they would gravitate to playing songs from their current
passion project.

Lasky was impressed with what he heard and invited Meredith over to his
office. When Meredith arrived to the meeting, Lasky held a copy of Meredith's
book *And There I Stood With My Piccolo* in his hand as he shared his big idea
about *The Music Man* with Meredith.

Jesse had the idea to make a documentary film titled *The Big Brass Band*
that would tell about the tremendous band activities in U.S. schools. The film's
hero would, in the course of the story, form an All-American Band selected
through local contests, consisting of the two best instrumentalists in every
state, the result being a crack hundred-piece outfit. Jesse told Meredith he
was actually going to form such a band and had already put the organization
into place through bandmasters and music educators throughout the United
States. He wanted Meredith to write a march for the climactic finale to the
film. And while Meredith was certainly excited and flattered to be asked for

the assignment, he'd hoped for some sort of solid interest on Lasky's part for *The Music Man*. So he invited Lasky to his home to hear more of his score and script that he and Rini would perform for them. Lasky happily accepted the invitation, and a few days later, he was sitting in Meredith and Rini's living room enjoying hearing a performance of the latest version of the show performed by his hosts. Meredith said, "He was a happy audience and enthusiastic about the picture possibilities."[6]

"Let's pair up," said Lasky. "Stick the projects together and see what happens." They shook hands on the spot, and then brainstormed on how to seamlessly connect the two projects. Might Harold Hill have a grandson to bring the audience up to the present day to bridge the two ideas together timewise? The evening wrapped up with smiles and enthusiasm all the way around. And then, in great Hollywood fashion, a week later, Meredith heard from Lasky again: "The periods and the ideas have nothing in common, and we'll end up ruining *The Music Man*, which already strikes me as too long," Lasky opined. But all was not completely lost. Lasky continued:

> My idea would be to do two pictures—produce a double feature. I don't think a "program" production like that has ever been done. *The Music Man* would start the bill and *The Big Brass Band* as a straight documentary would finish it![7]

Meredith was buoyed by this latest approach. And because both he and Lasky did business with the same agent, they called their representative and asked him over to Meredith and Rini's house for a time when Meredith and Rini would perform the show yet again. And not only did the agent bring himself but also fourteen other possible investors.

Rini and Meredith performed a somewhat cut version of the show, which, even so, "seemed to take three days" according to Meredith.[8] During the entire presentation, there wasn't a sound in the room—not a laugh, not a chuckle, "not even a snick," added Meredith. And no reaction at all to the songs. "Jesse tried a few prop reactions in the beginning, then just sat there in the corner as pale as a ghost, completely gagged by the fantastic silence that froze every vibration in the room except my voice droning on and on. I wanted to quit a dozen times but didn't know how. Rini got so mad she could hardly see straight and sang like an angel."[9]

Exit, Stage Right, Jesse L. Lasky.

Meredith and Lasky did remain loosely in touch, however. And not too long following the flop living room presentation of the show, Lasky did indeed complete his *Big Brass Band* documentary, with none other than Jimmy Stewart narrating. However, there was no All-American Band formed for the film, which was the thing Lasky had his heart set on. "The more stumbling blocks he ran into, the harder he worked," said Meredith, "and he always came up smiling."[10] But Lasky's perseverance to finish the film successfully regardless of his obstacles inspired Meredith to keep pursuing his own passion project called *The Music Man*. But it was not going to be easy, and Meredith could still have no ultimate idea of the stumbling blocks that were ahead.

During summer 1956, the year that seemed to last forever for Meredith, Feuer dropped in on Meredith for a somewhat informal, in-person end-of-the-deal for Feuer and Martin to produce the show. Feuer told Meredith that he had his permission to use the title *The Music Man* for what it was worth and then waxed philosophical again on how excited he had been early on. Then, in typical Feuer idea-a-minute style, he had yet another possible angle for Meredith's show and asked to use the phone.

After a quick call, Feuer told Meredith to go immediately to Hillcrest Country Club. He had called producer Sol Siegel, who was currently producing *The Philadelphia Story* for MGM. Feuer said to me:

> I told Sol about the show and might he sit with Mere and chat about it. I figured he could help Mere lick the book. Sol produced a truckload of films, including *A Letter to Three Wives* and *Three Coins in the Fountain*—both nominated for the Academy Award for Best Picture.[11]

So off Meredith went to the Hillcrest Country Club to meet Siegel, where Meredith then invited him and his wife to his home to present the score and ad-libbing of the book. Sol and his wife "didn't leave till three o'clock in the morning—'starry-eyed' would not be too strong a word to describe the way they looked."[12] The Willsons bid the Siegels a happy good night (what was left of it) with high hopes for the show. Meredith sent Siegel the current draft of the script the following day. Siegel then called the next day after reading it and said he had already spoken to Bing Crosby, who was seeing his top representative that afternoon. Another twenty-four hours passed, and *The Music Man* seemed to at last be on the fast track, after four and a half years of development already. Then, a letter from Siegel arrived to Meredith:

> "Crosby interests not interested at this time." However, the message continued: "Still trying."[13]

Thirty days later the script was returned to Meredith by special messenger.

Exit, Stage Left, Sol Siegel.

But Hollywood is ultimately a small town in many ways, and word gets around. And word about the show soon reached hit radio show *Fibber McGee & Molly* writer Don Quinn.

Oops . . . Don has to go to Honolulu and is unavailable after all—another dead end.

Oz came a'calling next. *Wizard of Oz* Scarecrow Ray Bolger was encouraged by his agent to drop by Meredith's home to hear the score. Bolger loved the score. Then, Bolger was promptly signed for a full year of television to host a show titled *Washington Square*. Goodbye, Bolger, and any gravitas he could bring to the project to help lure a top-notch producer—end of that possible yellow brick road.

Meanwhile, Meredith continued to tinker with the book, trying to handle how to organically incorporate the disabled child and flesh out the character of Marian. Perhaps she's a schoolteacher and not a librarian? He rewrote everything to fit this premise, and it didn't work.

Things weren't looking good for Marian . . . or any of the "River City-zians."

August 1956 had rolled around by now. Meredith and Rini were so numb from reading the different versions of this *Music Man* to each other they were paralyzed on the subject. But August would bring a surprising new and needed twist to the show that would help change its trajectory for the better.

Fate and Franklin Find a Way

Meredith had agreed to write and conduct the music for *The California Story*, a large-scale dramatic/musical pageant in San Diego "with thirteen hundred actors and two thousand horses (Rini says every time I tell it, I add a couple hundred horses)."[14] The two-week gig offered him and Rini the chance to take a welcome break from working on the show nonstop for now five years. So off they went to San Diego for Meredith to work on this California pageant extravaganza. The Willsons promptly met the man who was adapting and troubleshooting the script for *The California Story*, named Franklin Lacey. Lacey was "a six-foot four skinny, extrovert of a homemade apple pie smile on stilts . . . like we'd known him all our lives."[15] By the end of their busy two-week stay in San Diego, the musical event was a big hit and a needed morale booster for Meredith and Rini. And they had bonded with Franklin Lacey.

Twenty-four hours after the pageant's final performance and cast party, Meredith and Rini were visiting with Lacey in the afterglow of the success of the pageant telling him their *Music Man* and Feuer and Martin stories. And although Meredith had enjoyed a needed break from actively writing on his show during the intense work on *California Story*, he had still brought the two-feet-high manuscript stack from *Music Man* just in case the creative muse would visit while he was in San Diego.

Getting his head out of the show to focus on a completely different project had given him the needed objectivity to "partly narrate and partly read the story to Franklin with some considerable enthusiasm."[16] Meredith explained further:

> "Professor" Harold Hill was still The Boy; Marian, the Librarian, was still
> The Girl. The janitor's [disabled] son was still the subplot. Mayor Shinn was
> a kind of heavy, his wife Eulalie was the scatter-brain social leader of River
> City; Charlie Cowell, an anvil salesman, was emerging as Harold's envi-
> ous rival, Tommy, the "Kilroy" juvenile, and Zaneeta, the Mayor's apple-
> of-his-eye daughter, were still the sub-love story; and the crochety school
> board still became an inseparable barbershop quartet as Harold Hill's first
> "miracle" in River City. As I look back now, with the simple elements I
> had from practically the very first draft, it seems almost impossible that I

> could have spent so long a time cluttering up this simple story instead of
> clearing it up. But then you don't know how glued I was to the [disabled]
> boy subplot—how badly I wanted to tell on stage that [such children] are
> muscularly [disabled], not mentally [disabled].[17]

Lacey was a welcome audience of one . . . listening intently, laughing and crying
in all the right places. As it turned out, he was not only a former stage manager, "play doctor," playwright, and former child-prodigy lecturer but also an
adjunct professor at a private California college where there were some disabled children enrolled. Therefore, he was the first real sympathetic listener to
the script who supported and respected the disabled child subplot. He said, "I
can wade you through this jungle overnight. I can see how the scenes should
follow as clearly as if I was seeing this show on the stage!"[18]

The rest of that day with Lacey was spent playing the game of now-you-
tell-me-the-story-of-*The-Music-Man*-in-the-fewest-possible-words. Meredith
and Rini had played that same game for years with everyone and anyone who
would listen—including their dog, Piccolo, and cat, Cookie—honing and selling the plot. This technique is called by some producers an "elevator pitch" (see
if you can tell the basic story of your show by the time you reach the next floor
before your prospect gets off).

Lacey became the secret sauce to taming the book that Meredith had
needed for a long time. His objectivity, and especially his knowledge of stagecraft and dramaturgy, were just what the show doctor had ordered.

Meredith had also learned a system from Ernie Martin of "drawing" scenes
visually by representing each one with a different-sized rectangle. For example,
a small horizontal rectangle indicated a scene downstage near the footlights.
Then, Meredith would draw vertical rectangles on top of the horizontal one
to indicate where the song(s) happened in that scene. By hooking all the rectangles together, one could instantly see a visual flow of the show with dialogue versus songs, and where the dialogue took place on the stage. Franklin
would point out stagecraft methods where one could, if necessary, follow one
full-stage scene with another without necessarily having to always arrange a
smaller scene in-between to allow the stage crew time to change the scenery.
Today's modern Broadway theatre with its much more advanced staging and

scenery techniques available, including sophisticated projections, would render some of Martin's approach useless. Nevertheless, the flow of a show (songs versus dialogue) still could benefit from this sort of "planogram" today.

With Lacey fully on board and totally committed to helping, Meredith and his system of shaping and trimming the book had evolved into a well-oiled machine/routine:

> I would write all day and Franklin would come over at around four or five o'clock and I'd scream and holler the scenes I had put down on the paper since yesterday. And he'd scream and holler enthusiastic agreement or enthusiastic disagreement. Then one way or the other, I'd worry about it during the night, sleep some, and make changes and go ahead till four, five o'clock the next afternoon. The signal to stop was when Franklin banged on the door. Then the hollering would begin again. In this manner I got a completely new draft written down on paper, final-typed in carbon, too.[19]

During one of those "hollering/screaming/banging on the door" days, Meredith wrote what would become a classic moment in American musical theatre, known the world over.

It was September by now, a little over a month since Meredith had met Lacey. And in Meredith's "constant preoccupation with cudgeling the brain for authentic recall,"[20] he lit into writing one of his priming essays about the "evils" of pool halls and some similar social scourges of 1912. As he wrote and wrote, this new essay grew into a lengthy diatribe, and before he knew it, Meredith had applied his lyric writer's ear to a large chunk of dialogue without consciously intending to do so. He figured this pool hall speech he had written could pass as a good lyric in the show, with its rhythmic feel. Meredith wrote, "Its words fell trippingly off the tongue without consonant bumping into consonant and without any embarrassing non-sustainable syllables showing up at the ends. And it didn't rhyme!"[21]

So Meredith created—of all things—a musical accompaniment to this speech—not a tune with a melody but a piano accompaniment. As any writer can tell you, when you're "in the zone" and things are clicking, time flies. Such was the case with Meredith at this point writing Harold Hill's signature opening number:

> I want to tell you that I've had days go by fast, but that day when Franklin
> hammered on the music room door and I hollered "tomorrow," I'll swear
> it seemed like he just stepped back from that door and hammered again—
> that's how fast tomorrow came even though I did go to bed.[22]

With Franklin and Rini standing by, Meredith "jumped onto the piano and ad-libbed the rhythm accompaniment, no melody, and hollered, "Well ya got trouble" at my good friend Franklin, "right here, I say, trouble right here in River City." And he didn't stop for the whole six-page harangue. Rini, who'd been hearing it for two days, stood there beaming; their dog, Piccolo, was "barking her brains out," said Meredith. Even their cat, Cookie, "deigned to turn her head passing by the door." Their secretary, Joan, grabbed the paper as he finished and began typing the lyrics like mad.[23]

Meredith had reached another hallmark turning point in the show, and he—and Rini, Franklin, Joan, Josephine, Piccolo, and Cookie—could feel it, too. The immortal "Ya Got Trouble" had been birthed, and musical theatre would never be the same. It became the signature "speak-song" moment in the show among other such moments and was technically the first rap ever heard on the Broadway stage.

Thanks to my visits with Rosemary Willson, at one point I stood in the very room in that Brentwood, California, home where Meredith first performed "Ya Got Trouble." Rosemary even generously allowed me to play a few notes on the same piano Meredith first banged it out in front of his small audience that day. And the energy still vibrated in that space! The room now contained various bits of memorabilia given to him from fans of the show: a miniature River City main street (complete with a pool hall); pictures hanging on the walls of productions of the show from around the world; and another picture with Meredith and President John F. Kennedy when Meredith was awarded at the White House by the president the Big Brothers/Big Sisters of America Award. The walls and piano were talking—and singing—to me on that day in that room, and I could almost hear Piccolo barking.

October now came to Meredith's evolving show as the year-that-never-seemed-to-end kept unfolding. But there was clearly a new and exciting wind beneath his wings in writing and shaping it. Then one day, housekeeper

Josephine did something she never did and came barging into Meredith's music room with the door shut while he was "hunting and pecking" on the typewriter. She announced that a Mr. Martin was at the front door. The only "Mr. Martin" in Los Angeles Meredith knew was Bill Martin, who was on the board of directors of the Big Brothers/Big Sisters of America organization. But why would he be dropping by unannounced?

Rini, having heard the chatter between Meredith and Josephine about this Mr. Martin, came out with the cold cream she had on her face and curlers in her hair. Who could this impromptu visitor be? Josephine was given the okay to open the door as Meredith and Rini eagerly awaited. The door opened.

"Hi, Rini. Hi, Mere. You got anything to drink?" said Ernie Martin.[24]

Mr. Martin was happily ushered into the Willson Home as Rini excused herself to remove the curlers and cold cream. Meanwhile, Martin proceeded to tell Meredith he'd tried to reach him on the phone in advance, but the line was busy and couldn't get through (call waiting was clearly still a thing of the future at this point).

"Ever hear of a book called *Indian Joe*?" said Martin. "Book-of-the-Month-Club a couple of years back."

He went on to explain that him and Feuer had obtained the rights to the book and were going to produce it as a film with MGM. But they also had their sights set on a Broadway musical version of the property. Martin proceeded to tell Meredith that he and Feuer had considered several first-rate composers to write the score for a stage version of *Indian Joe*, including Cole Porter and Irving Berlin. But they had decided Meredith Willson was their number-one choice ("Cy keeps saying you're the best words-and-music man in the business," said Martin). They already had procured a theatre (not a small feat, to say the least) and were ready to go into rehearsals by August of the next year (1957). He added to Meredith, "Here's your chance to learn about Broadway from the top in a guaranteed hit with everything solid gold all the way: The best writer, Book-of-the-Month story that's news, the best company, theatre, backing, everything top-drawer, top-notch, top-grade."[25]

Meredith was gobsmacked. But he still wanted to handle taking care of Martin's earlier request from his initial entrance. So he served him a glass of tonic, and then they got down to business.

"Pretty flattering the way you bounced me up at the head of the list there. Those other names you threw at me were not chopped liver, you know," Meredith said.

Martin continued to pitch the *Indian Joe* project with gusto, but Meredith wanted to talk about *The Music Man*.

Meredith continued, "Well, you thank Cy for me. And you tell him I've got some new rhymeless wonders like The Train I'm anxious for him to hear. [But] I don't see how I can do this *Indian Joe* project with you guys. I got a project, remember?"

"You mean *The Music Man*?" replied Martin. "I thought you gave that up."

"I didn't," Meredith replied. "You did."

"You mean you licked the book?" he said.[26]

Meredith immediately pulled him into the music room, seated him in a chair, and proceeded to "turn on his word sprayer," as Meredith called it, and "spray" Ernie with Act One, Scene One (draft number thirty-two). This included important, new material that Ernie hadn't heard yet. By now, Rini had joined them, sans cold cream and curlers. And she and Meredith didn't stop until the curtain dropped on the Act One finale, which, at that time, was Harold Hill singing "The Sadder But Wiser Girl" on one side of the footbridge and Marian on the other side singing "My White Knight" simultaneously (clever and perfect in helping highlight those characters' psyches in that moment as that was, it was decided later in the evolution of the show that a big choral, full-cast number—"The Wells Fargo Wagon"—was the right way to end the act while revealing a slight thawing of the ice in Marian's disdain of Harold).

After Meredith and Rini finished their impromptu performance (Act Two was not finished yet), Martin was genuinely impressed. But he was still not backing off his offer for Meredith to write the score for *Indian Joe*. He told Meredith that even though Act Two wasn't finished yet, he and Feuer would produce *The Music Man* in 1958. But in the meantime, they were busy and committed to the other property. And eager for Meredith to get started on it.

"Wouldn't you rather have two Broadway hits than one? Learn about Broadway from the top? A major musical comedy . . . with all the top people in the business? At least come over to my office and let me outline the show for you so you'll know what you're turning down," pleaded Martin.

Meredith agreed to do so but with mixed emotions. Still, he had nothing to lose but a meeting time with Ernie.

"I spent practically the whole next day in Ernie's office," wrote Meredith. The premise Martin pitched to him was "irresistible" (well, almost). But Meredith held steady. He told him he had "too much steam up on *Music Man*" and that he couldn't just walk away from it. "Can't turn it off that fast. Can't get intense enough about some other completely different kind of a show just now. And if I can't get intense about it, how can the stuff I write be any good?"[27]

At this pivotal moment in the life of *The Music Man*, my conversation with Feuer fills in the gaps.

> I had told Ernie we couldn't let Meredith slip away on writing this new show for us. Therefore, Ernie told Meredith to not make a hasty decision, even though his passion was clearly with *The Music Man* at that time. Ernie told him to not answer him then . . . but to talk it over with Rini. Take his time. Call us in three weeks with his decision.[28]

So, Meredith agreed to call Feuer and Martin three weeks from that upcoming Monday around 11:30 a.m. or 12:00 noon at the latest with his decision.

Would *Indian Joe* cause Harold Hill and Marian the Librarian's fates to be changed? Eliminated? Or delayed? And what would happen to them in Act Two? There was no Wells Fargo wagon to come rolling into town to save the day at this point. The song hadn't even been written yet.

Ten

THE GARDEN BLOOMS
WITH BLOOMGARDEN

Meredith who?

—Kermit Bloomgarden

I t is *still* 1956. Approximately seven years had now passed since Frank Loesser had phoned Meredith to suggest he write a musical comedy. Let alone the time that had passed since Meredith and Rini performed the three-hour-and-forty-five-minute early draft of *The Silver Triangle* for Cy Feuer and Ernie Martin. Meredith had been "tilling the soil" of his musical for years, with some "sprouts" that had sprung up here and there with it, but still no production to show for his efforts. He was still looking for the breakthrough that would cause *The Music Man* to blossom into full flower.

Meredith had a solid offer from two of Broadway's top producers to write the score for what they thought would be their next hit musical, *Indian Joe*. And he had bought some time with Feuer and Martin to think it over. And as a part of his "thinking time," he sought the input from trusted friends. Some of his friends thought getting away from *The Music Man* project for now, or perhaps dropping it altogether because it had gone nowhere up to this point, was the right thing to do.

"Grab it, Mere," said one. "Do the *Indian Joe* show now . . . look at the Broadway experience you'll get, with the absolutely top guys," said another. "You so rich you can turn down a guaranteed Broadway Feuer and Martin musical comedy smash hit?" added another. His friends reminded him of the financial success a Feuer and Martin hit could bring through playing a major theatre on Broadway, then a road tour, then a cast recording, sheet music, and performance income through ASCAP. Maybe even a film version! "Grab it, man, grab it!" said the chorus of voices.[1]

But Meredith continued his Iowa stubbornness, and still held on hope that *The Music Man*, his passion project, could yet get off the ground with the right producer. And then Rini, in her inimitable Russian accent and occasional awkward use of the English language said to him early in the three-week think period, "Darling, I sure don't want to stir you wrong, but I say to heck with [*Indian Joe*]. You finish *The Music Man*."[2]

So Meredith did just that. He finished *The Music Man* on a Monday. At 11:45 a.m. Pacific Time.

The second act was done . . . at least a first draft of it. He now knew what became of that loveable rogue Harold Hill . . . and Marian the Librarian—and more. And it was completed on the day that he was to call Feuer and Martin with a decision.

While the day was still young, at least on the West Coast, Meredith had a stroke—of genius. At the time, it seemed like a simple, passing, shot-in-the-dark thought. But it would eventually prove to be much more than that.

"Rini, you know Frank Loesser's bit hit musical *Most Happy Fella*? It's produced by a guy named Kermit Bloomgarden. Wonder if he'd be interested in producing *The Music Man*?"[3]

The Most Happy Fella had opened earlier that year in May to excellent success. But that it—a musical—was produced by Bloomgarden was a bit of an outlier because he seldom ventured into the treacherous waters of musical comedy. Sure, Bloomgarden by 1956 was a well-known Broadway producer with a solid track record of successful play productions to his credit (*Death of a Salesman*, *The Crucible*, *The Diary of Anne Frank*), but he was not known for producing musical comedies, *Happy Fella* notwithstanding. Accordingly, had Meredith told his friends about this latest idea of approaching Bloomgarden, they might have thought his Iowa stubbornness had guided him in the wrong direction.

Meredith had ten minutes left before keeping his promise to call Feuer and Martin. Why not try to locate Kermit Bloomgarden? Meredith tells the story:

[Bloomgarden's] office located him in a theatre some place. I could hear rehearsing going on. "Hello, Mr. Bloomgarden!" I says, hollering even louder than I do in a room. Now Cy and Ernie have a rapid-fire delivery, but we Hawkeyes yield to no one when it comes to being long-winded. I unreeled the whole story to Mr. Bloomgarden about Ernie and Cy asking me to do the score for their new show, about Ernie expecting my answer today, about my just finishing the new draft, about my friends' opinions, about my agent's opinion, and after quite a while when I stopped for a breath Mr. Bloomgarden said, "Pardon me, have we ever met?"[4]

Meredith admitted that, indeed, they had never met, but Bloomgarden's interest was evidently piqued. He requested Meredith send him a copy of the play. But Meredith (wisely) resisted because he knew there were a lot of unique numbers, such as seven salesmen imitating the sound of a 1912 train with their rap-like nonrhyming speech. Let alone "Ya Got Trouble." Without a spirited performance of those pieces, they tend to sit on the page with no real life.

"Fine," said Bloomgarden. "I'll give you all the time you want any night this week."

Meredith suggested Wednesday, and Bloomgarden agreed. They would meet at Broadway musical conductor Herb Greene's apartment at 200 West 58th Street in New York City.

At midnight.

"Why midnight?" Meredith asked. "That will give Herb a chance to get home from conducting *Most Happy Fella*," replied Bloomgarden. Meredith thanked him, hung up, and called Ernie Martin.

"Well, I'll be doggoned," said Ernie. But never-say-die Ernie urged Meredith not to completely turn down *Indian Joe* just yet. "[Bloomgarden] may not like your show. He may not like you. You may not like him. Lots of things can happen. Cy is in our New York office. Go see him Thursday morning after you do the audition." Meredith agreed but hastened to add he wouldn't be there early Thursday morning since his audition didn't begin until midnight.[5]

The Audition of a Lifetime

Meredith and Rini hopped on the next plane to New York and were sitting in the Waldorf Astoria hotel that Wednesday, waiting for midnight to arrive. Eagerly anticipating their next presentation of the show (which, by now, they had done countless times), they arrived a little early to Herb Greene's apartment. They were ushered into the space by Herb's wife. They walked past framed posters of hit Broadway shows Herb had conducted: *Guys and Dolls, Can Can, Silk Stockings, The Most Happy Fella,* and more. Meredith secretly wondered if *The Music Man* poster would ever hang on that same wall.

Not long after Meredith and Rini had taken their seats, in walks Herb Greene with his "curly dark hair, extrovertism in his white leather coat with a large dill pickle he was eating like an ice cream cone."[6] Herb happily greeted Meredith and Rini and then pointed him to the piano. Soon thereafter the doorbell rang, and Kermit Bloomgarden was ushered into the room, and Meredith and Rini laid eyes on him for the first time:

> [He was a] well-proportioned nice-looking fellow very well dressed. He said Hodado and that was about all. It wasn't much of a night for talking— sleety, cold, blowy outside, and painful, nervous, tense and a little unreal inside—at least it was for me. December 19th it was, 1956. I'm always nervous at the beginning. If all goes well right off, I get over it. If not, I lose my courage and start collecting that cotton in the mouth. Cotton mather, I call it because that's what it feels like—mather.[7]

Bloomgarden brought several people from his office with him that night. And with it being such an unpleasant night weather-wise, the pleasantries were short. So after the brief preliminary chatting, Meredith and Rini got down to business.

"Curtain up," said Meredith, after simulating an overture on the piano with a few chords. He shot one last glance at Bloomgarden. "He favored me with what I have since learned is legendary in the trade," said Meredith. "'The Bloomgarden Look', which, according to [playwright] Thornton Wilder for one, [that look] would 'tunnel through an Alp.' I breathed in and started with The Train."[8]

It was silent and seemingly hostile in the room for the first several lines of "The Train" . . . until Herb Greene happily laughed out loud with "a yelping belt I'm sure you could have heard in Carnegie Hall a block down the street," said Meredith.[9] The sleety night of the New York ice had been broken. And Meredith's mouth started to moisten quickly as he and Rini proceeded. Then, Herb's genuine enthusiasm about what was unfolding in front of them seemed to catch on naturally with the others in the room. The ten-minute break they took between acts didn't slow anything down. Bloomgarden, Greene, and everyone in that apartment were falling in love—whether they knew it or not in those early morning hours—with *The Music Man* and its charms. Three and a half hours after Meredith had first shouted "Curtain up!" he then exclaimed "Curtain!"

> Herb and Kermit and everyone else, along with Rini and me—and my soaking sweaty shirt—were hugging and hollering and slapping backs and laughing and screaming all at the same time. And then Kermit and I really got acquainted. Two pounds of sturgeon and a couple dozen bagels later [Rini and I] left just as it was starting to get light.[10]

Later in the unfolding of the life of *The Music Man*, Bloomgarden admitted that when Meredith first phoned him that day to pitch his show to him, he didn't recognize Meredith's name. Bloomgarden revealed, "I said to myself, 'Who the hell is Meredith Willson?' It had been so long since I heard him on the radio, I'd forgotten all about him."[11]

Meredith and Rini took an early-morning cab ride back to their hotel, happy and smiling and feeling as if they were in some sort of dream state. But they had been down a similar road before with Feuer and Martin, so although they were elated, they were cautiously elated. The phone rang early the next morning at 9:00 a.m. It was Bloomgarden.

"Good morning, Meredith," said a sharp, clear, and evidently wide-awake Kermit. "Woke my wife last night when I got home, breaking a rule of a good many years. Had to tell her about last night. She got so excited we ended up in the kitchen with scrambled eggs and I haven't been to bed yet. Can you come over? I'm at the office."[12]

Meredith and Rini got the sleep out of their eyes pronto. A Broadway professional was calling who was still genuinely excited about their show the morning after the night of sturgeons and bagels. They readied themselves quickly to get over to Bloomgarden's office. But finding it for the first time was a little tricky at first because it was located behind a great block-long sign on Broadway that hides the second floor where Bloomgarden was located. Meredith and Rini finally found a small pair of doors behind the box office of the theatre building in which the office was located ("You almost had to buy a ticket to get in," said Meredith). In they went, as Meredith said to Rini, "If we're not on Broadway now, this is about as close as we'll ever get."[13]

Meredith was knocking on the doors of Broadway at just the right time. The so-called golden age of the industry was in full swing. The 1940s had seen hits such as the seminal, groundbreaking *Oklahoma!* (1943). Then others dazzled audiences: *On the Town* (1944); *Carousel* (1945); *Annie Get Your Gun* (1946); *Brigadoon* (1947); *Finian's Rainbow* (1947); *Kiss Me, Kate* (1948); and then another triumph for Rodgers and Hammerstein before the end of the decade: *South Pacific* (1949). The 1950s were equally stellar and dizzyingly successful: *Guys and Dolls* (1950); *The King and I* (1951); *Can Can* (1953); *Kismet* (1953); *Wonderful Town* (1953); *Peter Pan* (1954); *Damn Yankees* (1955); *Silk Stockings* (1955); *Li'l Abner* (1956); *The Most Happy Fella* (1956); and the beloved *My Fair Lady* (1956). To say Meredith had hard acts to follow would be an understatement.

And yet, ticket prices and production costs were rising, and television threatened to erode theatre audience attendance. Still, Meredith was ready for the next step, if there was going to be one at last.

Several Bloomgarden staff members entered the room as Meredith and Rini took a seat on the couch in Bloomgarden's office. A quiet fell over the room as Bloomgarden cleared his throat and said "it":

Meredith, may I have the privilege of producing your beautiful play?

Perhaps Meredith was thinking in the back of his mind at that point:

There were bells on the hill, but I never heard them ringing.
No I never heard them at all,
Till there was you.[14]

Eleven

HOMEGROWN MAGIC

I always think there's a band, kid.

—Professor Harold Hill

Before Meredith could give Bloomgarden a solid answer to Bloomgarden's offer to produce his show, he had a promise to keep with Feuer and Martin. And that was to run over to their office on East 52nd Street to give them the final shot at producing the show. Meredith and Rini hoofed it over to the office ("too excited to sit in a cab" Meredith said).[1] They soon arrived, and Cy Feuer was waiting for them with bated breath.

"Kermit's going to do it, Cy," Meredith blurted out immediately.

"He said so?" shot back Feuer.

"He sure did," answered Meredith.

"If he said he'll do it, he'll do it," responded Feuer. "You'll get a top production from Bloomgarden. I think he'll do your show better than we could," he added.

Bloomgarden's reputation was solid in theatre circles, and if he said he would produce your show, "you can now tell your friends," according to Meredith.[2]

Feuer, Meredith, and Rini embraced. Said their goodbyes. And that was that.

Meredith and Rini hoofed it back to Bloomgarden's office and ecstatically told him that he was the official producer of *The Music Man*. Smiles, handshakes, and hugs all around.

"Now, we have work to do," said Bloomgarden.[3]

Meredith had to be thinking at that point, "Work? What have the last several years I've poured into this show been?" But he didn't say that. He rolled up he sleeves and got to work. But he had a solid foundation on which to fine-tune, and in some cases, overhaul his show.

Meredith's solid foundation were the characters on which his show was built. Characters that were synthesized, combined, and melded from folk whom he'd known growing up in Mason City, Iowa.

Meredith's mama, Rosalie, had befriended Alvin Tank, the kid whom Meredith saw in the boys' band picture, which inspired him to make the show about a boys' band. Tank became the (eventually redeemed) juvenile trouble-maker Tommy Djilas. The last name Djilas came from a Bulgarian ex-patriot who worked in one of Meredith and Rini's favorite New York delicatessens. The wheelchair-bound boy Meredith envisioned in the show (still in it at this time) eventually morphed into a lisping child named Winthrop who was still internally grieving his father's sudden death. Winthrop was based on young Charlie Haverdegraine, a lisping harmonica player from Mason City. Meredith said that, as a child, he begged his mama for a harmonica "because it seemed so much easier to play than a flute." He added he got the idea that Charlie could play the harmonica because he lisped. So a young Meredith said he tried to get Charlie to teach him "not how to play the harmonica, but how to lisp."[4]

There were other characters whom Meredith still had work on which to do, but their foundations were solid: The Irish Mrs. Paroo, Marian the Librarian's mother, was based on the Willson's housekeeper, Mrs. Buehler (of German descent). And the pool hall commotion grew from Meredith's home church's organist Ed Patchen's trips to Mason City's Pleazol Billiard Parlor to play the dignified game of billiards that had no "evil" pockets in the table. Mason City's B. F. Goodrich Tire Store manager, Marcellus Washburn, found immortality as well since that became the name of Professor Harold Hill's sidekick. Numerous locations in the show, such as the footbridge, were also direct references to actual places in Mason City. Not to mention countless references of places and things from the era in which the show is set (i.e., Dan Patch, Cap'n Billy's Whiz Bang, noggins and firkins, bevos, cubebs, Sen-sen, etc.). This all added to the true authenticity of the show, while transporting audiences back to 1912 Iowa. But what of Harold Hill himself? Where did he come from? Before the opening of *The Music Man* in 1957, Meredith wrote in a newspaper essay on the show, "Harold Hill is so many people that I remember different ones every time I see the show."[5]

Meanwhile, back at the Bloomgarden office, Meredith, Rini, and Bloomgarden and company were engaging in the delicious exercise of projecting who might play the titular role in the show. Names such as Danny Kaye, Dan Dailey, Gene Kelly, Ray Bolger, Milton Berle, Art Carney, Jason Robards, and Jackie Gleason were all tossed around . . . and on the names came flying. But there was one role and name that was yet to be filled for the show. The most important name of all. The director.

"Morton DaCosta or Moss Hart, either one would certainly be great for the show," said Bloomgarden. "Moss lives in my apartment building," he added.

But the holidays were on them at this point, so they all agreed to table serious discussions and an approach for the director until the next month in early January. Meredith and Rini lunched with Bloomgarden and his wife, Ginny, then parted to return to Los Angeles as they would with close and dear friends, even having only known each other for less than twenty-four hours. Talk about an instant connection. *The Music Man* had worked its magic once again of bringing people together.

Two weeks later, Meredith and Rini were back in New York, ready to audition the show yet again. This time for the purpose of finding the right director. The time and place were set: Once again at Herb Greene's apartment ("for good luck," said Meredith) at 9 p.m.[6], where Meredith and Rini had presented the show to Bloomgarden a few weeks before. Unfortunately, with Greene still conducting *The Most Happy Fella*, he couldn't attend, and Meredith said he would "miss the big laughs Herb gave before."[7]

Bloomgarden had a habit of inviting any and all friends whom he ran into the day of an audition to see it. Accordingly, crammed into Greene's apartment were approximately twenty industry people sitting everywhere possible— including Moss Hart and his wife, the glamorous actress, singer, and champion of the arts, Kitty Carlisle.

Phenomenally successful playwright and director Moss Hart had just come off of his triumphant direction of *My Fair Lady* (which was still in the midst of its successful Broadway run). So when Moss and Kitty entered the room, everyone sat up a little straighter in their chairs.

The audience was warm, especially after having been there for four and a half hours after 9 p.m., when Meredith finally hollered "Curtain!"

Everyone was gracious but ready to exit at that early morning hour of 1:30 a.m. Moss said he liked the first-act curtain; Kitty had reacted happily and absorbedly. But at the end, Mr. Hart had only three things to say: To Rini, "You sang very prettily." To Bloomgarden, "Phone you in the morning." And to Meredith: "Good night."[8]

The morning after, Meredith's hotel phone was ringing at 9 a.m. It was Bloomgarden. He started talking about a song Meredith had told him about that he might want to put back into the show.

"What did Moss have to say?" Meredith eagerly asked.

"Moss? Oh, he didn't like it." Bloomgarden then barreled along to the next topic. But still curious, Meredith stopped him and asked, "What didn't he like about it?" According to Meredith, Bloomgarden then answered "Who?" And Bloomgarden continued to barrel along with *The Music Man* in the weeks ahead, never looking back at Moss Hart . . . and thinking of who their first-rate director could be to helm the show. During that process, he got the show in front of a lot of the movers and shakers on the Broadway scene of 1957.

"Don't do it, Kermit," the Broadway intelligentsia told him. "It's corny. And you'll never fix that book."[9] But Bloomgarden was a man of his convictions and keep pressing forward.

Rini waxed philosophical to Bloomgarden on the Moss Hart snub:

> So I sang "very prettily," did I? Well, I say the Lord had His arms around us when Mr. Famous Moss Hart turned us down, Kermit. Do you know what he hung in the closet that night at Herb Greene's? A *mink-lined* overcoat. What would he know about small-town Iowans like us?[10]

Bloomgarden had his hands full with finding the right director and somehow talking Meredith out of the disabled-boy-in-a-wheelchair subplot. Meredith was finally coming to terms with what had to happen along these lines:

Kermit spoke mainly about my considering getting rid of [the boy]. Kermit knew he had to go, but he also knew the way to lose him was not to give me an ultimatum about it—he knew that just digging that subplot out of there would leave a pretty raw hole. Also, he understood my strong feeling about [the boy] and how important I felt it was to the play. So he never told me for sure we had to lose the kid, preferring to let me find out for myself. However, I suspected I was in for the empty paper bit, possibly even Act One, Scene One a few more times. If I'd known how many more—well, I'm glad I didn't.[11]

Meredith and Rini knew they had to move to New York and get an apartment so they could be close to the action. They found one on Central Park South and had a piano brought in. Meredith was working hard on the disabled child subplot, plus cutting a good forty-five minutes from the still too-long show. The calendar rolled over to February and Bloomgarden had yet another audition for Meredith and Rini to do for some "important people" including a gentleman named Morton DaCosta.

Tec Time in River City

Born Morton Tecosky in Philadelphia, Pennsylvania, in 1914, Morton DaCosta (nicknamed "Tec"—pronounced "Teek") began his career as an actor in the Broadway production of Thornton Wilder's *The Skin of Our Teeth* starring Tallulah Bankhead in 1942. A decade later he made his stage-directing debut with *The Grey-Eyed People*. DaCosta had a string of hit Broadway productions as director prior to meeting Meredith: *Plain and Fancy, No Time for Sergeants*, and *Auntie Mame*. DaCosta once said, "The job of the theatre is not to feed pessimism but to dispel it."[12] With the overall optimism of the show that Meredith had created, it looked as if there might be a perfect match here.

So on another cold night in New York City, this time in Bloomgarden's apartment, Meredith and Rini geared up for this latest audition of the show. They had never met DaCosta, so they didn't know who that night in the crowded room might be DaCosta. Meredith described the occasion:

> You'd think no audition would have been tough after that first night at Herb Greene's. How could there ever have been any more at stake than there was that night? Any audition should have been a breeze after that. But it doesn't work that way. Every audition is a world unto itself—microcosmic. And everyone in it is ditto. The afternoon of this particular one I even considered rehearsing with a real piece of cotton in my mouth—I swear the thought crossed my mind—to see if I couldn't get used to performing that way, just in case.[13]

Meredith took his place at the piano with Rini next to him. They recognized hardly anyone in the room, but Bloomgarden had told them in advance that, in addition to DaCosta, there were a few other successful directors sitting in, along with a few famous Broadway set designers who might show up . . . Howard Bay and Jo Mielziner. "Oh, and an angel or two"—potential investors, casually added Bloomgarden. Plus, to top it off, several theatre owners, because there are a limited number of theatres on Broadway and if the theatre owners don't like what they hear, you don't get a theatre for your show, even if you have everything else in place. Meredith was definitely starting to feel cotton mather gather inside his mouth by now. At that moment, Rini who had slipped away to the kitchen unnoticed by Meredith, appeared and put a glass of water for him at the piano. Then, a tall man with slightly gray hair walked over before things commenced.

"Hello, Meredith. I'm sore at you."

This jolted Meredith out of his preoccupations with his cotton mather preperformance jitters. The gray-haired man continued.

"Every morning at eleven o'clock. Don't you understand? I was a 'listener dear.' Every morning at eleven I shaved while you gave me my Beethoven lesson on the radio. And what did you do? Took me up to *Symphony Number Eight* and cast me aside like an old glove."

"Well, the program folded," said Meredith, preening and purring.

"That's no excuse," shot back this stranger. "You should have continued anyway. Changed my whole life!" Seems one of Meredith's radio shows about classical music turned this gentleman into a new, classical music lover. Bloomgarden was now calling the room to order.

"Uh, thank you and see you later, Mr.—ah—?"

"Shubert," he replied. "John Shubert."[14] Only the proprietor of what Meredith and Rini and said would be a perfect theatre for their show . . . the Majestic Theatre on 44th and Broadway (the home for the last thirty-plus years of what is now the longest-running musical in the world, *The Phantom of the Opera*).

"Ladies and Gentlemen, I present to you Meredith and Rini Willson and *The Music Man*," proudly announced Bloomgarden. Polite applause as Meredith hollered, "Curtain up!" He and Rini launched into the show. But thanks to his relaxing exchange with Shubert, cotton mather was nowhere to be found. And after a thirty-second faux overture, the train was soon chugging along:

> Meredith
> Ya can talk, ya can talk, ya can bicker, ya can talk,
> Ya can bicker, bicker, bicker, ya can talk, ya can talk.
> Ya can talk, talk, talk, talk, bicker, bicker, bicker,
> Ya can talk all ya want but it's different than it was.
>
> Rini
> No it ain't, no it ain't, but you gotta know the territory![15]

In between and during singing, playing, and speaking, Meredith was scouring the room. Which person could possibly be DaCosta? Is it the tall, angular man who's not smiling at all? Uh-oh, another Moss Hart who's not really enjoying it. "Okay, forget about him. He's probably just a deadpan," concluded Meredith. He decided to play instead to the blond guy directly in front of him, who was enjoying himself like a relaxed friend of the family. "He probab'ly *is* a friend of the family. Must remember to ask Kermit to invite this blond guy all the time" thought Meredith.[15] Meanwhile, Shubert was still laughing it up, totally enjoying the show.

Before they knew it—because they were so accustomed by now to performing this still-too-long show—Meredith was hollering, "Curtain!" and that was that.

Applause, smiles, laughter all around. Except from the one person Meredith and Rini had most wanted to impress—Morton DaCosta. He hadn't smiled nor chuckled once during their performance. Talk about trouble in River City.

Meredith and Rini stepped into a nearby bedroom for a moment so Meredith could change into a dry shirt. Rini gave him a small rubdown and kiss. As they came back into the room, DaCosta already had his coat on and the door in his hand to leave. He finally spoke.

"Great. Best thing I've heard. Like very much to do it. Good night!"

As he was starting to walk away, Meredith grabbed his shoulder and said, "*Hey!* That's *wonderful!* But wait a minute, Mr. DaCosta." The gentleman turned around to speak.

"Bay," he said. "Howard Bay. Sets, lighting—all like that. I'm late. Good night."

So right before their eyes, one of the most successful set and lighting designers of the era (*Show Boat, Finian's Rainbow, Man of LaMancha*) had signed up.

At that moment, Bloomgarden pulled Meredith and Rini back into the thick of things and introduced them to his stellar guests that evening: Bob Fosse, Joe Anthony (*Most Happy Fella* director), top director for stage and film Vincent Donahue, investor G. M. Loeb . . . and about a dozen more. But still, no DaCosta. He had not even shown up!? Some last-minute change of plans, most likely. Turned out DaCosta's agent told Bloomgarden he wasn't going to ask DaCosta to come that night. Material is too corny, heard the agent. Besides, DaCosta's already committed.

Well, at least Rini had struck up a conversation with the pleasant blond guy who laughed it up in front of them. Rini brought this nice man over to meet Meredith. He glowed about the show.

"Congratulations. I don't know when I've heard anything fresher or more charming. Your lyrics are highly original, and I love those excursions into dialogue in rhythm. What do you call those?"

"Speak-songs, I guess," replied Meredith. "Glad you liked them." Meredith tried not to sound too crestfallen since DaCosta had fallen through. Who knows, however. Perhaps one of the other directors in the room will sign on. Who needs DaCosta anyway?

"Darling," Rini said. "This is Morton DaCosta."

"*Hey,*" said Meredith. "That *wonderful!*"

"I'll be seeing you, Meredith," said DaCosta. "Very soon. Good night, Rini."[16]

And no sooner had DaCosta exited the room than Meredith and Rini soon found themselves in another early-morning-floating-on-air cab ride back to their hotel. In that one evening, it appeared their fledgling show had garnered a premiere theatre, top-notch set and lighting designer, and a successful, solid-gold director. It was almost too much to take in.

The following morning, DaCosta, Meredith, and Rini met in Bloomgarden's office. DaCosta was as enthusiastic as ever about the show and firmly stated his desire to direct. He did indeed have to clear some things from his calendar, but he was happy to do so. But DaCosta expressed his concern about the book: "It's a little long," he said. "And the disabled child I think should go." Bloomgarden jumped in: "Meredith's working on that . . . trying to sneak up on it instead of just tearing it out."

Meredith nodded. But he still had no idea on how he could excise the subplot that meant so much to him. Let alone trimming the show more and more than he already had cut. He could possibly hear Cy Feuer and Ernie Martin whispering in his ear, "That book's going to be hard to lick, Mere." Or other voices possibly danced in his head: "Stay away, Kermit. This corn will never sell."

But then, none of those people had ever met a neck-bowed Hawkeye whose mama had taught him about perseverance and focus back in Mason City. Or experienced John Phillip Sousa's rigid discipline. Or the fire of Arturo Toscanini's baton. And practicing his cross-hand piano exercises on a bitterly cold Iowa morning. Looks like some fancy maneuvers and intestinal fortitude were needed once again to keep moving ahead to pull this show off. But Meredith had the goods inside. And he could already see that band.

Twelve

THE PLOT-AND
CHARACTERS-THICKEN

I try to write about certain simple, sentimental facts of human beings that
are understandable and not discouraging or depressing.

—Meredith Willson

Although Meredith Willson never explained in his writing or otherwise
why his original title for *The Music Man* was *The Silver Triangle*, it stands
to reason the "triangle" was not only emblematic of a band but also the triangle of Harold Hill, Marian the Librarian, and her brother Winthrop. Or perhaps the triangle consisted of Harold, Marian, and music itself. In any event,
in this chapter, I explore the three "sides" of the triangle: Harold, Marian, and
Winthrop—why their respective evolutions through the years of Meredith's
journey writing *The Music Man* were worth the wait and what makes them
immortal characters on the musical theatre landscape.

Winthrop Paroo

Ableism, or the presumption that someone who appears to have a disability is less intelligent than others, was obviously a driving force in Meredith's
thoughts about an important message he wanted to communicate in *The Music
Man*. It was certainly a noble and needed message to be communicated, not
only in 1957 but always. It is unknown through Meredith's writings or connecting the dots otherwise as to why this was an important mission for him. But
a hard-fought mission it was through multiple drafts of his show and one he

would not easily release. But eventually, with the input and solid guidance of Cy Feuer and Ernie Martin, Kermit Bloomgarden, and then Morton DaCosta, Meredith knew the boy in a wheelchair subplot had to be removed or somehow transformed so as not to distract the focus of the musical's love story, nor its theme of the transforming power of music. Through the creative process, careful guidance from some Broadway professionals, and as referenced in the previous chapter regarding Meredith's lisping, harmonica-playing Mason City childhood friend Charlie Haverdegraine resonating somewhere in his subconscious, Winthrop Paroo was finally born. He arrived at breakfast in Rumpelmayer's Restaurant in New York City on a snowy day.

Meredith was still meeting and consulting with Franklin Lacey, and at that Rumpelmayer's breakfast, Meredith was waxing philosophical about "Broadway magic." He was referencing the scene to Franklin in *My Fair Lady*, when Eliza Doolittle finally "gets it" through exhaustive training and speaks proper English for the first time, and the song "The Rain in Spain" erupts in a joyous celebration. Franklin replied, "Theatre magic like that works best when you least suspect it." Meredith agreed, pointing to what he thought might be bona fide theatre magic moments thus far in his own show:

> Like when the schoolboard guys sing their first barbershop chord after hating each other for fifteen years. There's some more theatre magic in our show you don't expect, in the first-act finale where the Wells Fargo wagon is coming down the street and the townspeople are so eagerly waiting for it—the spot where the lisping kid comes out of the crowd so excited he busts out singing "Oho the Wellth Fargo wagon ith a comin'." Here's this kid who isn't even identified. Just a lisping kid but you get hit with some magic anyhow. Imagine if the lisping kid were somebody we know—some character in the story—then you'd have some real . . .[1]

Meredith couldn't finish his sentence as Franklin Lacey was jumping out of his skin. According to Meredith, "spontaneous combustion" happened in that magic moment of its own in Rumpelmayer's. "A lisping kid instead of a disabled boy!" they said together. "Ashamed of his lisp—a big introvert problem child," Meredith said, then added, "Goodbye, disabled boy. I'll write a play about you someday, if it's the last thing I do."[2]

So as things developed with the show, the cast would eventually be in place (more of those delicious details later). However, the now wheelchair-freed, lisping Winthrop Paroo, brother of Marian the Librarian, ended up being the last and most difficult of the principal roles to be cast.

Bloomgarden, DaCosta, and Meredith had seen "nine million little Lord Fauntleroy professional stage kids" audition for the role, but still had no luck in finding the right child who would be an unpretentious natural in the part. That is, until Rini was watching one of her favorite television shows one night (the game show *Name That Tune*) and saw a ten-year-old named Eddie Hodges on the show. He'd become a contestant on the program and was paired with another contestant—future NASA astronaut John Glenn (at the time a military test pilot). Hodges and Glenn went on to appear on several broadcasts of the show. When Rini saw Hodges and his sparkling, natural on-camera personality shining through, she proclaimed to Meredith, "He's Winthrop. Positively, exactly!" She beckoned Meredith into the room to catch Winthrop . . . er, Hodges, before the show ended that week's episode. Meredith just missed him, but fortunately Hodges would be back on the show. After trying to get both DaCosta and Bloomgarden to also tune in the next two weeks for the show, they all finally saw him on an episode before he ended his stint with it. It was unanimous: This kid named Eddie Hodges seemed perfect for the role. A few phone calls later and he was summoned to the Imperial Theatre on Broadway for a daytime audition. "And when he walked out on that stage," Meredith said, "we got hit with a dividend you couldn't have told about from black-and-white TV: carrot-red hair!"[3]

Eddie Hodges got the part.

And it was not accidental that Meredith was looking for a ten-year-old to play the part of Winthrop. Since *The Music Man* is set in 1912, that was the year that Meredith was ten years old. He later admitted, "I suppose some of my points of view are reflected in the role of Winthrop."[4]

The red-haired Eddie Hodges is now white-haired and living in Mississippi. He is the only living principal cast member from the original Broadway production of *The Music Man*. I was able to contact him, and he was effusive in his praise of the show and Meredith and Rini Willson. "Being in *The Music Man* was an incredible experience," said Hodges. "Many of my memories have unfortunately faded by now about the show, but I will never forget Meredith and Rini Willson's kindness to me."[5] The role was clearly transformative for him. His time on Broadway led to a motion picture role with Frank Sinatra in Frank Capra's *A Hole in the Head* where, with Sinatra, he sang the song "High Hopes" (enter "Eddie Hodges High Hopes" in the YouTube search engine to enjoy their timeless, joyful performance. You'll see the unpretentious, red-haired, winning child that instantly enchanted Rini and Meredith on *Name That Tune*). Hodges had to leave the cast of *The Music Man* after a year with the production to make the Capra film, and from there he enjoyed a continuous stream of work in movies, television, and recording.

Robert Preston, Barbara Cook, and Eddie Hodges.
EDDIE HODGES PERSONAL COLLECTION.

Madame Librarian

Winthrop's basic character arc may have been in a good place, but other characters still needed a lot of fine-tuning. And as many of the lead characters continued to come into focus, it became more and more obvious how one-dimensional Marian now appeared. Just why was she so aloof from her fellow townspeople? And why was there no boyfriend by now in her life, let alone why she seemed to be a bit snobbish? Meredith said, "I had to locate her in a phrase. Then let her take it from there" to let the audience in on who she was. Meredith added:

> Her first-act song, the first version of "My White Knight"—was at that time in the form of a short introspective ballad, expressing her longing for the guy of her dreams. When we know exactly what kind of guy that is, we ought to know what we don't know yet about this girl. Her lyric in this song, so far, didn't tell us enough. It isn't a Lancelot she wants, nor a John L. Sullivan. She's not a snob either—she doesn't want any egghead necessarily, nor is she afraid of getting a little manure on her front porch from the local Iowa farm boys. Okay, we know all that. What else? Maybe she just wants a guy who is not too Iowa-Stubborn to love her and to admit it once in a while. A guy who is not ashamed of the few nice things she likes around the house. Like the Marble Faun and Emerson's Essays. A guy who, for example, is not ashamed of a few nice things. And there it finally sat—just like that. Fell into the lyric like a clam in the chowder.[6]

And with that one thought, Marian started to emerge:

> *Marian:*
> My white knight, not a Lancelot, nor an angel with wings.
> Just someone to love me, who is not ashamed of a few nice things.
> My white knight, what my heart would say if it only knew how.
> Please, dear Venus, show me now.[7]

He now added these new couplets to further flesh out what Marian wanted:

> *Marian:*
> All I want is a plain man.
> All I want is a modest man.
> A quiet man, a gentle man.
> A straightforward and honest man
> To sit with me in a cottage somewhere in the state of Iowa.[8]

Meredith had started to unravel ingenue Miss Marian with the fine-tuning of her "I want" song. "I want" songs are staples in the musical theatre canon for the hero, or heroine as it were, in this case. Such a song states early in the show what the protagonist(s) hopes for (and usually gets by the final curtain). Examples of classic "I want" songs include "Wouldn't It Be Lovely" (*My Fair Lady*); "Something's Coming" (*West Side Story*); "Some People" (*Gypsy*); "The Wizard and I" (*Wicked*); and "My Shot" (*Hamilton*). Perhaps Meredith's early musical theatre writing prodder, Frank Loesser, also provided an example and inspiration for Miss Marian with the protagonist ingenue Sarah Brown's song in *Guys and Dolls* where she also sings early in Act One about what she is—and is not—looking for in a love interest:

> *Sarah:*
> I'll know when my love comes along
> I won't take a chance.
> I'll know he'll be just what I need.
> Not some fly-by-night Broadway romance.[9]

But this was just the beginning of fleshing Marian out. She evolved into much more than the typical musical comedy ingenue. Unlike Laurey in *Oklahoma!* or Peggy Sawyer in *42nd Street*, for example, Meredith molded Marian into a strong, smart, fiery, complex young working woman. And for musical theatre in 1957, she was quite a revelation. Not only is she the town's librarian but she also teaches piano on the side. She is the sole provider for her family since the death of her father. Plus, we find out she has some baggage: She's an outcast in the community, and other ladies in River City gossip about her. But why? We are left to wonder until her hard shell first starts to soften ever so slightly at the end of Act One with the arrival of Winthrop's cornet delivered by the Wells

Fargo Wagon. But Marian's arc had still much to travel even until the final, climactic scene of the show.

But amid her tough demeanor to Harold Hill, we find out Marian is also a dreamer. In the quiet of the library, she lets herself get swept off her feet for a moment while she is momentarily under the spell of Harold during the "whispering ballet" (as Meredith called it), "Marian the Librarian." As a librarian, she has safely lived in the fantasy of her books. As a piano teacher, she is caught up in the emotional payoff of great music. But something has been damming up the flow of her emotions and realized fantasies to fully let go and be herself—to give and receive true love. She therefore has no suitors at this point in her life. And some of the songs she sings in Act One are not the only moments revealing what's going on internally with her. Early in Act One when she realizes Harold has convinced her mother into signing up to purchase a band instrument and uniform for Winthrop, she gives Harold a tongue-lashing. She lets him have it with the fact that her father is dead, leaving Winthrop brooding about it for two years, hardly speaking to others. How dare a charlatan, fake music professor such as Hill prey on her mom and fatherless brother, she reasons. She walks out in a huff. In that moment, we get our first clue of some of the things that are troubling her.

But Meredith allows us to see there's also a gentle heart beating beneath that fiery exterior when she sings in Act One both "Goodnight, My Someone" and of course, "My White Knight." These songs reveal how she fantasizes about her ideal man, but it's clearly *not* "Professor" Harold Hill.

How could a fly-by-night, gal-in-every-city con man such as Harold Hill fall in love with this spinster librarian, "stuck-up piano teacher"? For that matter, how could a womanizing gambler such as Sky Masterson fall for the buttoned-up Save-a-Soul "mission doll" Sarah Brown? And do so believably in a two-act musical comedy. Indeed, and fortunately for millions of consumers of such classic shows, this magic trick can be pulled off with the right song and dialogue construction, to say nothing of the talented performers in the respective roles to make such things plausible. And it's harder to achieve than it looks. Many have tried and failed. It took Meredith years, numerous script drafts, and several "ah ha!" moments to pull it off.

Marian's complete turnaround begins with Winthrop's conversion the moment he receives his "solid gold cornet" from the Wells Fargo Wagon at the end of Act One. Although Marian knows (with perhaps a reasonable doubt) that Harold is not a real music professor—after quietly researching some of his educational claims only to find they're bogus, she also realizes by the end of Act One he has indeed brought some happiness to River City. And most certainly he has brought happiness before her eyes to her troubled brother, whom no one else could seemingly do up to that point. By the final curtain, she realizes she doesn't need a "white knight" at all, but someone who can use the transforming power of music and belief to indeed deliver some magic and miracles to a community greatly in need of them, even the town's school board who has "hated each other for fifteen years." Even Harold Hill himself doesn't believe what he's selling during the show. Or does he? But more on him next.

During the years of working on the show up to this point, Meredith often stated he wanted to "get Mama in this show" one way or another through representing her somehow. He shared right before the Broadway opening of the show regarding Marian:

> I remember my childhood so well that each character in the show is not one, but a composite of three or four different people. One possible exception could be Marian Paroo, who is pretty exactly my mother, although I didn't realize it myself until [the show was in out-of-town previews].[10]

So Mama was in the show, after all. And why not? Rosalie Willson, with her proper upbringing, piano teaching, baggage she carried of a troubled marriage, and appreciation of "a few nice things" certainly pointed squarely in Marian's direction.

Professor Harold Hill

The musical theatre repertoire is filled with loveable, appealing con artists from its earliest roots to today: Gaylord Ravenal (*Show Boat*, 1927); Joey Evans (*Pal Joey*, 1940); Ali Hakim (*Oklahoma!*, 1943); Luther Billis (*South Pacific*, 1949); Starbuck (*110 in the Shade*, 1963); Bialystock and Bloom (*The Producers*, 2001);

Elders Price and Cunningham (*The Book of Mormon*, 2011); and Evan Hansen (*Dear Evan Hansen*, 2016). And on the list could go.

But there was never before, nor since, as appealing and beguiling a con man in the musical theatre canon quite like Harold Hill. Meredith debated with Feuer and Martin, Franklin Lacey, and himself if the audience should know Harold was a con man from the beginning of the show or if it should be revealed later. The former was wisely chosen because by letting the audience know of Harold's duplicity and selfish motives from the beginning, he would have to seduce the audience as well as the citizens of River City if he would earn his hero's stripes.

Harold has few redeeming qualities for most of the show: He makes a romantic play for the ultimately vulnerable Marian—the only person in town who could expose his fraudulent claim to be a music professor—simply to keep her off balance so she won't uncover his scam. He is ruining the reputation of other traveling salesmen in the territory because of his boys' band scheme. And he takes money for band instruments, uniforms, and lessons to form a band for which he is wholly unqualified to teach. As Harold's nemesis, Charlie Cowell, says in the opening scene, "He doesn't know a pipe organ from bass drum! He doesn't know *one note from another!*"[11]

But Harold is a "by-god spellbinder," according to Mayor Shinn. And the citizens of River City are soon taken with him not long after he's stepped off the train and figures out a need to create a boys' band, spell-binding the citizens with his evangelical oration that there's indeed "trouble in River City, with a capital 'T' and that rhymes with 'P' and that stands for pool!"[12] If that weren't enough, he closes the deal at the Madison High School gymnasium, where the good townsfolk have gathered for the annual Fourth of July opening ceremonies. Harold dons a band director's coat and hat on the spot and proceeds to spin a song about the time seventy-six trombones marched into town for a big parade along with some of the most famous bandleaders ever—of course, including the one-and-only John Philip Sousa. Talk about nerve! By the end of the number, everyone—sans Marian and Mayor Shinn—have "seen the band" and bought into the idea.

Harold sings his own "I want" song next in Act One to his sidekick, Marcellus Washburn, where he makes it clear he's not looking for any sort of "wide-eyed Sunday school teacher" (don't forget, Meredith's mama taught Sunday school). No, Harold is looking for "the sadder, but wiser girl" who's been around the block and wants no sort of happily-ever-after. This is a clear contrast to what Marian will sing later in Act One regarding what she desires for a "white knight" love interest. The two songs can actually be sung together (!) perfectly—again, no accident from Meredith—showing the contrast of their wants for a perfect half. If you can find a used copy of the recording Meredith and Rini made post-Broadway opening titled *And Then I Wrote* The Music Man, you'll hear Meredith and Rini perform the two songs juxtaposed on each other. It's an amazing moment if you've been familiar with the two songs for years.

In Harold, Meredith created a character that does all the above with effortless charm, clearly not only bringing the citizens of River City under his spell, but the audience as well. It took Robert Preston to first prove it could be done.

Late in the show, we are shown that Harold has an authentic side. It's revealed that he really does dream of being a band director but had given up on that dream years ago as "kid's stuff." And after he gets his salesman's foot in the River City door, it gets caught in that door because he has genuinely fallen for Marian. As previously noted, Harold and Marian learn, if only subconsciously, that although their wants are first at odds, they've been singing the same tune all along (literally, as noted, since the melodies for "Goodnight, My Someone" and "Seventy-Six Trombones" are virtually the same, just sped up for the latter). Harold and Marian both carried baggage around with them, and now they were ready to jettison it, come clean, and realize life never started for them "Till There Was You."

Although the power of love is strong enough to move mountains, is it strong enough to make the citizens of River City forget the fleecing they've received from Harold Hill? When he's hauled into the River City High School Assembly Room in the final scene of Act Two, it's doubtful at first. When Mayor Shinn reminds the townspeople of the money they've spent for instruments, uniforms, and lessons in exchange for the guarantee of a functioning boys' band which would get River City out of its "trouble," Iowa stubbornness rears its head and things look bleak for Harold. Then, when an actual ragtag group of boys comes unexpectedly marching in wearing uniforms carrying their instruments, we're clearly in for one of the most magical moments ever in the history of musical theatre.

Marian insists Harold conduct "his" band, but he resists—not only because he knows how bad it will sound—but also because he dare not try to really believe in himself as a conductor and fulfill his lifelong dream. The mask has finally been ripped off The Great Seducer.

Even when he doesn't believe in himself in that moment, he musters the courage to give that downbeat due to Marian's true belief in him, but first pleading with the boys to "think men, think"—a reference to how Harold had taught them using the "think system" where reading music wasn't necessary, only *thinking* the notes would make the music come out of their horns. What follows is an awful and painful rendition of "The Minuet in G" which they had "practiced" (by singing it) here and there throughout Act Two. But parents of the band members, seeing their children play instruments for the first time ever, are overcome with the pride that only a parent can feel when their child brings them their first, archaic, and crude piece of artwork: This is a masterpiece.

Perhaps Tommy Djilas, the young man whom Harold had temporarily put in charge of the band in his absence while he was planning his getaway, somehow found some time to do some actual semblance of rehearsing so the kids could at least produce at least this version of the song. But the parents and audience don't care. They, too, have seen the band, literally, and all is forgiven and well. Harold and Marian ecstatically embrace as the curtain falls on a happy ending.

The real music man, Meredith Willson, has pulled off the ultimate spellbinding on the audience through the silver triangle of Harold, Marian, and Winthrop. He has shown us *when there's music, belief, togetherness, and love . . . lives and communities can be transformed for the better.* And maybe even live happily ever after.

But there would be no transformations or happy endings to happen in 1957, or beyond for *The Music Man*, because the money wasn't completely raised for the show yet. Kermit Bloomgarden had his own magic yet to perform.

Young Meredith conducting.

Warsaw, Poland production of The Music Man *(1972).*

Meredith at his piano in his Brentwood home.

Meredith at his piano (1942).

Young Meredith joins the Sousa Band.

Meredith perfecting his "pucker."

"Wells Fargo" first draft lyric sheet.

Meredith's impromptu leading of his hometown band.

Meredith at the NBC microphone.

Meredith with Shirley Jones (left) and Dinah Shore.

President John F. Kennedy presents The Big Brother Award to Meredith.

Rosemary and Meredith Willson (1968).

Birthday time on The Music Man *film set (left to right, Rini Willson, Morton DaCosta, Shirley Jones, and Meredith Willson).*

The Greater Willson Family (Meredith is on the first row, third from left).

Thirteen

CASH AND CAST

Casting sometimes is fate and destiny more than skill and talent, from a director's point of view.

—Steven Spielberg

The days kept ticking away for the year 1957, and if Kermit Bloomgarden was going to get Meredith's show to land in Broadway's Majestic Theatre that year, there was still a lot of ground to cover. And securing all the financing was certainly job one at the Bloomgarden offices for *The Music Man*. Yet, Meredith and his show had already plainly cleared several unbelievable hurdles by now. But that didn't add up to an opening night with an overture. And cast. And sets and costumes. And pit orchestra.

During the so-called golden age of Broadway, when it was a different business in many ways, there could be one, two, or three names above the title as producer. In the current Broadway world, it is standard to see *three dozen or more* producer's names. The stakes were always high producing a musical on Broadway, but they're higher now than ever, it seems, due to the skyrocketing costs to create them and get them on stage. That's why you (unfortunately) seldom see a completely new musical (meaning original story and original music and lyrics) produced on Broadway today. Producers are looking for an existing property—most likely a film or best-selling book—that already has a trusted brand and, therefore, helps advance ticket sales and increase their odds of success. Most Broadway shows lose money, at least on the New York production. A road company can possibly help put a show in the profit category, but that's far from guaranteed. That *The Music Man* was not trading on an existing, familiar property made it all the more a gamble.

My Fair Lady was based on the hit play *Pygmalion*. *Fair Lady* had opened in 1956 largely through financing from television giant CBS. So Bloomgarden had CBS in his sights and had landed some brass from The Tiffany Network (as it was called in those days) to come and learn more about this new play from Iowan Meredith Willson. Accordingly, Bloomgarden had another backer's audition set up with about forty to fifty people present, and the four executives from CBS had the prime seats in his office to watch Meredith and Rini work their magic. And once again, the heat was on. DaCosta was there as well, but the material in his show wasn't quite as refined yet as Meredith wanted it to be. And with the CBS suits there as well, Meredith's nemesis cotton mather (in his mouth) came to visit, and his performance was a bit disastrous. As he described it:

> It was brutal. I just couldn't get on, that was all. Tried to ad-lib the story and got the last four drafts all mixed up. Tried to do the new piano-exercise scene I had just written and forgot the lyric. Tried to read it and couldn't find my place in the script. All in all I started over three times. And then quit. The silence was dreadful. Oh that silence. The only sound in the room was my dry upper lip refusing to slide down over my dry teeth. Well, the great silence was never broken either by my pleasant ad-lib good evening joke, or by "The Train," or "Trouble" or "Seventy-Six" by which time I was a broken-down derelict in a doorway, stuffed with cotton mather. The CBS people and most of the others left after a while. Very polite about it all.[1]

Bloomgarden was unfazed. He brushed it all off and said "Next!" This Broadway professional knew he would provide the core funding and would get the total he needed one way or another. So it was time to forge ahead with casting.

Barbershop, Barbara, and That One Named Harold Hill

Before *The Music Man*, there had never been a barbershop quartet on a Broadway stage, except in the days of vaudeville, which, of course, is not the same thing. Meredith knew the difference between "real" barbershop singing and simply throwing four singers together. He also knew in those vaudeville days, "a good barbershop quartet always stopped the show with regularity."[2] With *Music Man* being set in 1912—prime time for barbershop quartets—and Meredith himself having sung in barbershop quartets before (and the art of barbershop quartet singing having exclusive American roots), it was logical, if only to Meredith at the time, to add another dose of pure Americana with a barbershop quartet. Yet another first for *The Music Man*.

The Buffalo Bills were a barbershop quartet formed in Buffalo, New York, in 1947. They had gained the attention of Meredith and countless others when they won the 1950 Barbershop Harmony Society International Championship. They were contacted and soon contracted—the first to sign on to *The Music Man* cast. Next hired was David Burns as Mayor Shinn, then the key role of Marian the Librarian. (Burns would later gain even more acclaim playing Horace Vandergelder opposite Carol Channing in another hit musical, *Hello, Dolly!*)

Barbara Cook, native of Atlanta, Georgia, was visiting New York City in 1948 with her mother, trying to find work as an actress. She began singing at clubs and resorts and eventually landed an engagement at the famed Blue Angel Club in 1950. She made her Broadway debut a year later in the short-lived musical *Flahooley*. She landed another role quickly, portraying Ado Annie in the 1951 City Center revival of Rodgers and Hammerstein's *Oklahoma!* After some more parts in New York theatre and television, she created the role of Hilda Miller in the musical *Plain and Fancy*, for which she won critical praise. This led to her winning a lead role in Leonard Bernstein's 1956 operetta *Candide*. Although *Candide* was not a commercial success, Cook's performance established her as one of Broadway's leading ingenues.

When she was presented with the script and score for *The Music Man*, Cook happily signed on as Marian. She describes her first encounter with the show:

> I was blown away when I heard the score for *Music Man* at Herbert Greene's apartment. That was the first time I'd heard that rhythmic singing, that speak/sing dynamite rhythm that propelled the show forward like a train leaving the station, keeps gathering speed, faster and faster, until you

just surrender to the sheer glory of the movement. I really did feel all of that even when it was just Herbert singing at the piano. I was knocked out. People forget that Meredith was a conservatory-trained musician, having played in both the John Philip Sousa band and in the New York Philharmonic under Toscanini, and that training and experience showed.[3]

The Music Man was fortunate to get Cook, and as it turned out, she was fortunate to get *The Music Man*. But Marian needed a Harold, and although a lot of names had been tossed around for a while, it was time to get serious.

The early discussions—as far back as with Cy Feuer and Ernie Martin—had focused on song-and-dance men for the role: Ray Bolger, Danny Kaye, Dan Dailey, and the like. But when DaCosta piped up one day and suggested they not limit their thinking to song-and-dance actors only, Bloomgarden agreed that the person who plays the role should first and foremost be a fine actor. "Let's take our chances in being able to teach him to sing and move," said Bloomgarden. Other names then came flying fast and furious as Harold Hill possibilities: Milton Berle, Lloyd Bridges, Van Heflin, Art Carney, Jason Robards, Robert Preston, Laurence Olivier, Alec Guinness, James Whitmore, James Cagney, and Andy Griffith. Something magical, or prescient, or just plain inspired caused DaCosta to speak up and say, "I think we ought to talk to Bob Preston about playing Harold." Herb Greene jumped in, "He took a few singing lessons off me a couple years ago. He didn't stay with it too long." Bloomgarden now weighed in, "I don't think we should leave out any possibility. Let's look at him. Unless Meredith gets Danny Kaye."[4]

Danny Kaye was the team's top choice for the role and for good reason. He was a star: a singer, dancer, comedian, musician, conductor, and more. He was a Pied Piper that could certainly lead any town into a scheme. He was also particularly adept at physical comedy, pantomimes, and rapid-fire novelty/patter songs. Before being sought after for the lead role in *The Music Man*, he had starred in several notable Hollywood films. With his name on the marquee, that would be money in the bank.

Both DaCosta and Bloomgarden had made earlier overtures to him about the role, but with no success to even connect with the busy performer. It was now Meredith's turn to take a crack at him. So he called Kaye. He caught him in the MGM barbershop. Meredith had rendered "Trouble" for Sylvia, Danny Kaye's wife, some weeks before in New York. But during his phone chat with Meredith, Kaye was excited having just finished a date conducting the Philadelphia Symphony Orchestra, and Meredith couldn't get a word in edgewise. They concluded their cordial conversation when Kaye had to go. So Meredith called Kaye's wife the next day since she had liked "Trouble" so much. Perhaps she could get his full attention and share her excitement with her husband about this new musical. After a day of waiting to hear back from Sylvia, Meredith finally heard from her. "The part's not right for Danny," she says simply and directly. Meredith begged to differ, but "she got pretty sharp with me" and that was it. End of call.[5]

Winsome song-and-dance film star Dan Dailey was next. Meredith got Dan's manager on the phone, who made a date for him to come to Meredith and Rini's California home to hear the score. Meredith invited some supportive friends who were fans of the score to add to the excitement. The appointed time to present the show to Dan was at 2:00 p.m. Meredith described the event, "It was 2:45 and then 3:15. I called Dan's manager and at length it developed that Dan had had to go to Phoenix to look at some horses, planning to return in a private plane to keep our date. As far as anything I ever learned subsequently, from either Dan or his manager, Dan is still there."[6]

Perhaps Meredith was getting cotton mather in his mouth again, but now for a completely different reason. Who *would* and *could* be Harold Hill?

Three days later, Meredith got a call from DaCosta, who had reached out to Robert Preston of all people. It seems DaCosta had prepped Preston with the music for "Ya Got Trouble," who had learned it.

Robert Meservey Preston was born in Newton, Massachusetts. And by the time he was on DaCosta's radar for Harold Hill, he had appeared in several Hollywood films—mostly westerns and most notably in a Cecil B. DeMille film *Northwest Mounted Police*, which one critic called "DeMille at his most ridiculous." Preston himself said of his film career, "I played the lead in all the B-pictures and the villain in all the epics. After a while, it was clear to me I had sort of reached what I was going to be in the movies."[7]

Meredith was unimpressed with the idea of Preston as Professor Harold Hill. Who knows, perhaps Dan Dailey would emerge from his Phoenix trip at last or Danny Kaye would have an epiphany that he'd made a terrible mistake and the role was indeed for him. Making a reference to *Northwest Mounted Police*, Meredith said to DaCosta: "You talking about Robert Snowshoes Preston, half-brother of Chingachgook, and inventor of the igloo and the aluminum dogsled?" *That* Robert Preston?

"I've got five words for you, Buster: Wait. Till. You. Hear. Him," shot back DaCosta.[8]

Bloomgarden would hear Preston do "Ya Got Trouble" later that day, and he was pleased. So Meredith told them to have "Snowshoes Preston" hop on a plane to Los Angeles as soon as possible and perform the number for Meredith. But Meredith was still skeptical. He had never met Preston and had only seen him in the B-grade films with which Preston was associated for so much of his career. Forty-eight hours after Meredith's phone call with DaCosta about him, Preston was walking through Meredith and Rini's front door in California, ushered in by Bloomgarden.

"Bob is my name," Preston said simply. "Shall we get acquainted now or later?"

"Whatever you say," replied Meredith.

Preston took off his coat and walked over to the piano. Meredith gave Bloomgarden a quick "Hello," sat at the piano, and hit an E-flat octave.

With that, Robert Preston then disappeared into Harold Hill with:

> Well, ya got trouble, my friend.
> Right here, I say trouble right here in River City.[9]

And that was it. Preston never looked back and never missed a beat. And for hundreds of performances of *The Music Man* on Broadway—and eventually the Warner Bros. film version—Preston never missed a beat. Meredith and team had found their Harold Hill at last. And the musical theatre would find an iconic character that would be heard around the world for generations to come, thanks to Robert Preston.

As Meredith said of Preston's Broadway production performance:

One of the greatest rewards of *The Music Man*'s story is that it released Bob
Preston from the wrong identity he had been strait-jacketed in throughout the greater part of his career. How this leprechaun of a volatile-witted
seventh son of Thespis' most lighthearted and most happily gifted seventh
sons could have been chained for so long in the ambling black-bear mas-
querade that not only obscured his true abilities but showed him, alas all
too convincingly, in complete—and unfortunately, highly successful—
juxtaposition to everything his great gifts clamored to really reveal—
remains one of the fascinating mysteries in the world of the theatre. Watch
him as night after night he gives you an opening-night performance in the
most glittering polish a role could ever hope to receive.[10]

But what about the additional money that Bloomgarden needed to raise?

Money, Money, Money

With Frank Loesser being the earliest encourager of Meredith to write such a
show, Loesser stepped up to the plate and sank in some substantial dollars, also
in exchange for a percentage of the music publishing rights for the show. This
made sense because Loesser's Frank Music Corporation was an established
publisher of Broadway songs, including those contained in his own creations
such as *Guys and Dolls* and *The Most Happy Fella*. Then, the show's musical
director, Herb Greene, felt as if he knew a hit when he saw and heard one.
So he, too, put some money down. There would be others who would invest
smaller amounts, but clearly Bloomgarden, Loesser, and Greene would profit
handsomely in the decades to come.

With Harold Hill, other principal cast members and financing now firmly
in place, it was time for Meredith and Rini to get back to New York, where
things were moving quickly for an open casting call for the chorus members.
It was starting to appear that things were proceeding toward that downbeat of
a conductor's baton for an overture and a show after all these years. And those
tough New York critics would have their say about the proceedings as well.

Fourteen

THE FINAL MARCH TO BROADWAY

The first production meeting for *The Music Man* glistened with a special kind of professionalism I've never run into anywhere else.

—Meredith Willson

Most people seem to always be able to remember and tell about—in great detail—their first car, first date, first teacher, etc. Meredith Willson wrote three shows that made it to Broadway, but in September 1957, he was experiencing a series of firsts with his first-ever Broadway show: the first production meeting, first costume sketches, first scenery sketches, first readings of scenes from his (still-developing) script, and the first chorus auditions . . . all at a blinding pace. It was almost too much to absorb. The writing and development of his show had taken years—with more than forty rewrites that still weren't finished yet—but now things seemed to be moving at warp speed. A note went out from Bloomgarden's office:

Kermit Bloomgarden
1545 Broadway
New York 36, NY

RE: The Music Man *Production Schedule*

Auditions:
September 5–Thursday . . . Open Call,
Dancers: 1:30 p.m. (Imperial Theatre)
September 6, 7th and 8th . . . Open Call,
Singers: 11:00 a.m.–1:30 p.m. (Imperial Theatre)
September 9–Monday . . . Equity Call,
Singers: 9:00 a.m. (Imperial Theatre)

The open call auditions were soon finished, and the chorus of singers and dancers was chosen, with contracts sent out in the weeks afterward. September then melted into October. The first official rehearsal (the read-through) was held on October 9. As they had done seemingly countless times before, Meredith and Rini performed the show, but this time for the full cast, which was a welcoming audience.

But behind the scenes, Kermit Bloomgarden was doing what producers do: raise money. And *The Music Man* was still not fully capitalized at this point. The good news was that Bloomgarden's track record of success preceded him. After all, as noted before, he had hits such as *Death of a Salesman*, *The Lark*, *Diary of Anne Frank*, and *The Most Happy Fella* under his belt. But it was October, and the show was scheduled to open on Broadway in December. So time was of the essence. Rules and regulations regarding raising money for Broadway shows are specific and complicated. Therefore, to cut legal expenses and delays, Bloomgarden restricted those who could invest in the show to New York State residents. But this eliminated a large portion of Bloomgarden's usual "go-to" investors from Connecticut and other states. There was also a business recession and unstable stock market at the time, which only exacerbated Bloomgarden's challenge . . . yet another big hurdle for the show to clear. Meredith had heard stories of Richard Rodgers and Oscar Hammerstein having to conduct approximately eighty (!) auditions for investors to launch *Oklahoma!*, and Meredith was dreading the road still ahead in that department. And yet, Bloomgarden was a total pro and never bogged his writer down with such extra concerns. As Meredith put it:

> Kermit never bothered me with finance. He figured I had my own problems. That point I would never argue. How he [raised the money] I still don't know. I do know that Rini's and my good friend from NBC days, Ken Banghart, came in with a syndicate group he organized; so did Sylvia Drulie, an associate producer; and I found out later that [musical conductor] Herb Greene raised $50,000 the hard way—a couple hundred, a hundred, even fifty, at a time—from friends and relatives.[1]

Meredith's "own problems" consisted of getting a final version of the script, once and for all, to the Bloomgarden office where Bloomgarden was "screaming" for it, according to Meredith.[2] While writing an original story and script offered its own challenges, each new script version resulted in a domino effect that caused some songs to be cut and others added. Every songwriter has a "trunk": songs that were written for whatever purpose months or years ago that never found a home and therefore were abandoned at the time but not forgotten . . . and therefore went into "the trunk." Meredith explains:

> I should say two or three [songs for the show] came from the trunk. All in all I wrote some forty songs, twenty-three of them between the opening of *The Silver Triangle* in Cy Feuer's apartment and the opening of *The Music Man* in the Shubert Theatre in Philadelphia. The final musical score as of the New York opening consists of eighteen not including the bits and pieces, and the ballets. Twenty-two numbers got cut, each one embracing the triumphs and disasters inescapable in the struggle for a beginning, middle and end, each song two small plays unto themselves—one entitled "words" and the other "music." Plus a three-page reprise for Mayor Shinn: "Ya Got Trouble, Mr. Hill," and a complete version of "Seventy-Six Trombones" with ancient instruments.[3]

"Till There Was You" was from the trunk—originally titled "Till I Met You."[4] And there were some fifty-three experimental "rhythm poems" Meredith wrote in his attempt to substitute rhythm for rhyme. "Ya Got Trouble" and the opening train sequence were the two "biggies" that made the final cut.

At last, the final working script was put neatly between two covers and a hundred copies were made for the cast and production team. Draft number forty-something.

On Your Toes

Once a show has had its read-through, the next step is blocking it—getting the actors out of their read-through chairs with the director giving the actors their stage movements. This is called getting a show "on its feet." This was now happening with *The Music Man*, as the actors were then starting to memorize their lines; rehearsal pianists were in place; and the music and dance rehearsals had begun in earnest. The Broadway rehearsal machine was up and running, with professionals at every turn. Veteran Michael Kidd's assistant choreographer from *Guys and Dolls*, Onna White, was making her debut as the lead choreographer for a Broadway musical. As White created the choreography for the show, she was assisted by seasoned pianist/arranger Laurence (Larry) Rosenthal, who created the dance arrangements for the show. And all of this was happening at a rehearsal hall on Second Avenue in New York City, only a few months away from their scheduled Broadway opening at the Majestic Theatre on 44th Street. The excitement was palpable for Meredith and Rini:

> The actors were getting their lines down now. Every day something new and exciting for Rini and me, like it was the first day in the world. Tec was calmly every place at once. Tec in a small banquet room setting up the book scenes—Tec in the ballroom setting up the production scenes; Tec with Herb in a lodge room down the hall hearing the singers, discussing movement and business and attitude. So many heart-stopping "firsts" during those [rehearsal hall] days. Herb called me in on the second day and knocked my hat off with that whole bunch belting "Iowa Stubborn," "Seventy-Six Trombones," "Wells Fargo Wagon," and "Shipoopi," pretty well polished and nearly half-memorized already.[4]

Also according to Meredith, Onna White was "taking charge like a veteran her first time out on her own. No panic, no hysterics—thinking out steps and routines, with Larry Rosenthal creating the arrangements at the piano without a moment's hesitation, bar by bar."[5]

The Music Man was officially on its feet and possibly starting to grow its wings.

But the creation of a musical is a highly collaborative process—one of the most collaborative of any art form. And after White had created her choreography, DaCosta would see it, suggest changes or some new routines, and the whole or partial structure would be torn down and re-created in the same painstaking, bar-by-bar process. And the dancers would then be required to remember the "old" steps with the newly added ones. Did it work? Did it not? If it was right, they knew since it had a certain "inevitability" about it.

And while the choreography was being carefully constructed, DaCosta was creating all the attitudes and movements to reflect the character of each and every "River City-zian" in the opening "Iowa Stubborn" number and beyond. Even the chorus members in River City had backstories, although the audience would never have known those stories from watching the show. Those stories and attitudes were reflected in DaCosta's careful direction with every flip of the hat, eyebrow twitch, and hand movement.

Nine days after the first rehearsal, on the tenth morning at ten o'clock, DaCosta gathered the entire company up from the lodge halls, pantries, banquet rooms, hallways, and lobbies and corralled them into the main ballroom for the first time since Meredith and Rini had done their version of the show for the cast. DaCosta addressed the cast:

> Good morning, ladies and gentlemen. From the top.[6]

Two hours and forty-five minutes later, Meredith had seen his show presented for the first time. Rosemary Willson described his excitement:

> He was elated. And he was amazed at the speed which the actors had absorbed and memorized the material so quickly, and so well. There was certainly work that still needed to be done, but to him, this felt like the start of something big.[7]

Meanwhile, as a part and parcel of a new Broadway musical, negotiations were soon to begin as to which record label would get the rights to record the original cast album. In 1957, there were "the big four" record labels: Capitol, RCA Victor, Decca, and Columbia. Whichever company offered the highest money advance and royalty rate for the project won the contract. In the case of *The Music Man*, three of the big four weren't even interested. It was Meredith's favorite of the big four—Capitol Records—that got the contract, which didn't even require an audition of the show (Meredith had to do one for RCA, Victor, and Decca). Capitol had seen though not heard the score and immediately put an offer on the table. And there was a serendipitous connection with Capitol Records for Meredith: A young man named Stuart Ostrow was assigned to help shepherd the project through to completion. Ostrow had met Meredith during his Armed Forces Radio (AFR) days, as Meredith had helped provide Ostrow an entrée into AFR. Ostrow described Meredith as "a consummate musician, pianist, composer, lyricist, conductor, and performer. He could write marches, barbershop quartets, speak-songs, ballads, and occasionally an aria, such as 'My White Knight.'"[8] Ostrow would later go on to produce and direct Meredith's third Broadway show, *Here's Love* (now titled *Miracle on 34th Street— The Musical*). So, Capitol Records became the record label for the show's cast recording (which would be recorded after opening night). The music business is littered with miscalculations, and *The Music Man* original cast album is one such for the "records" (pun intended) for RCA Victor, Decca, and Columbia. The album was released on January 20, 1958, and held the number-one spot on the Billboard charts for 12 weeks, remaining on the charts for a total of 245 weeks. The album received "Best Original Cast Album" at the first-ever Grammy Awards ceremony. In 1998, the record was inducted as a Grammy Hall of Fame winner.

Back at the rehearsal hall, surprises were still emerging, such as the Buffalo Bills barbershop quartet needing another song in Act Two. So Meredith left the rehearsal hall and did what he often did when he wanted to get his creative juices flowing: He walked. And walked. After a few false starts, he found a doorway to the song:

> I was trying to get in an old-fashioned mood which required considerable concentration walking alongside Park Avenue's glass and aluminum skyscrapers. So I concentrated on Mama. If I can't get Mama into the show any other way, I'll get her in a song.[9]

Thinking about his mama, Rosalie or "Rose," as she was sometimes called, led to him thinking about one of her sisters, Lida, who was his mama's favorite sister. So the (now-classic) barbershop quartet song "Lida Rose" was born as Meredith walked the streets of New York City. The Buffalo Bills sang the song the next day at rehearsal, and DaCosta and company loved it. And they were right. The development of the show and discoveries such as this during the show's period at the downtown rehearsal hall was akin to today's workshop productions.

Workshops were born out of a part of the developmental process of a musical somewhat accidentally with the show *A Chorus Line*. In it, creator/director Michael Bennett had a vision of a musical centered on the experiences of chorus dancers. So he gathered a group of dancers/performers to discuss their experiences and used a tape recorder to capture their stories. These stories were later transformed into a full-length musical with music by Marvin Hamlisch; lyrics by Ed Kleban; book by James Kirkwood Jr. and Nicholas Dante. This led to other shows, after a read-through, having workshop productions wherein rehearsals take place that allow plenty of room for the developmental process with the show's creator(s). This leads to an invited audience (or sometimes a publicly ticketed event) to see the show on its feet performed for the first time in front of a live audience. The current workshop process can be less expensive overall than the process musicals went through during Broadway's golden age. But the result is the same: It is determined through such a "tryout" period whether a show should make it to Broadway or not. As noted in this book later, Meredith's fourth and final show, *1491*, did not make it out of California and on to Broadway past its tryout period.

So after what was, in essence, *The Music Man*'s "workshop" period at a downtown rehearsal hall with the cast scattered throughout the building rehearsing, it was time to move the show "uptown" to a real theatrical space. The Majestic Theatre was in their sights, but it was not time yet for the Majestic. The New Amsterdam Theatre on 42nd Street was the cast's next stop.

Getting the Show on the Road

Today's New Amsterdam Theatre is a glittering, state-of-the-art facility leased and operated by the Disney Theatrical Group. After its 1997 Disney renovation, it was first home to the smash hit *The Lion King* and then *Aladdin*. But in 1957, the New Amsterdam was shoddy and outdated, a mere shell of its glory days when from 1913 to 1927, it was the home of The Ziegfeld Follies. During that era, stars such as Will Rogers, Fannie Brice, Eddie Cantor, and Al Jolson graced its stage. The legendary Follies producer Florenz Ziegfeld Jr. maintained an office in the building, which also contained a roof theatre. This was an actual theatre space, unlike where the cast and production team had worked prior. It was in this space where *The Music Man* would experience its next birthing stage. It was where Meredith and company saw the show for the first time in a true theatre perspective. But after a few days of rehearsals in the New Amsterdam, it was time to move again, this time four blocks up the street to the Barrymore Theatre on 46th Street.

Bloomgarden's staff distributed two hundred tickets to the company for the "gypsy run-through" of the show at the Barrymore. This term was used during Broadway's golden age to describe the final run-through of a show before it hit the road for an out-of-town tryout production, before hopefully returning to New York and Broadway. Through the long history of Broadway, there have been shows that "closed out of town" due to bad reviews or other problems before making it to Broadway. Such a "gypsy" run-through had no costumes, sets, or orchestra. Yet it's a fully staged presentation with the essentials of tables, chairs, working props, etc. Meredith describes the final moments before that first gypsy run-through:

> Tec had saved the last hour before the run-through to polish up the march-on curtain call to the music of "Seventy-Six Trombones." He always keeps a company occupied almost up to curtain time to keep them from worrying.[10]

With the curtain call march ready to go, the doors of the Barrymore Theatre were opened for the two hundred invited guests.

And in marched more than nine hundred people.

Meredith and Rini could hardly get into the theatre. Broadway was there in full force: producers, stars, directors, playwrights, composers, lyricists, recording executives, music publishers, CBS executives, NBC executives. "Everywhere you looked was a household word and his brother," said Meredith. "Rosalind Russell with her husband, Freddie Brisson, were in our row. Cy Feuer was just behind. Vincent Sardi, Greer Garson, Van Johnson, Harold Rome, Lawrence and Lee, Comden and Green, Paul Osborn, Frank Loesser, June Havoc . . . "[11] and on the list went.

After a brief introduction and welcome to the audience, noting his surprise of the audience's size, DaCosta then said, "This is our first run-through. We hope you enjoy *The Music Man*, ladies and gentlemen." He smiled, then added before he exited the stage, "Please be kind."[12]

The show was off and running with only a piano—no orchestra, no scenery, no lights or costumes. No curtain—just practice clothes, folding chairs for scenery, and a piano. And there sat all of Broadway watching, some expecting a total disaster.

But the magic of *The Music Man* delivered.

As Meredith described that first public performance of the piece:

> The reactions and laughs came fast and furious. "Iowa Stubborn" worked big. Then came "Trouble." Bob Preston was electric. "Seventy-Six Trombones." We can't believe any part of this. Rini looks at Ginny Bloomgarden who is leaning forward, her mouth ecstatically open, her eyes wide and shining, her face wet with tears. Rini grabbed her arm. "Does it always happen like this?" she whispered. Ginny shook her head without taking her eyes off the stage. "God, no," she says.[13]

For the "curtain call" (with no curtain), the piano started playing "Seventy-Six Trombones." The dancers appeared playing their pantomime trombones, and the audience burst into spontaneous clapping to the rhythm of the music.

Afterward, Meredith and Rini worked their way through the crowd to speak with Bloomgarden, DaCosta, Preston, and Barbara Cook. They were all elated and cautiously very optimistic. Who couldn't be after such an experience? And yet, even Broadway novice Robert Meredith Willson knew that once you add costumes, scenery, orchestra, etc., the beautiful simplicity of a show can get bogged down and lost fast, and fall on its face on a Broadway stage. The Broadway intelligentsia (at least a few of them) were already predicting the show's failure, and Meredith overheard them as he exited the theatre. The leading "potentate of pessimistic prophecy" was holding court.[14]

> "They'll never make it. Sympathetic audience like today is a pushover—who doesn't love Preston and Cook in that crowd?" he pontificated.

And then, as Meredith called it, the sage "ticked them into oblivion."

"One: where are the jokes? Two: the book is corny while the lyrics are too smart. Sure, they went over today with this crowd but the public won't get it—won't want it—even if they hear it, which they won't when there's an orchestra in the pit. No dice, gentlemen, no dice."[15]

Then, others chimed in with whispers the following day:

"Discount that terrific audience. That's not the guy who pays [for a ticket]."

"Costumes, scenery, orchestration, all those things slow a show way down as often as it build it up."

"A lot of those people yesterday wanted you to fall on your face, sure, that's par. But when the emotions start like they did, right off the bat, they'll forget themselves and go along with the poor bastards up there on that stage. They're all show people under the skin."

"The people who buy tickets have gotta be shown. And did you ever hear about critics? *They'll* tell you if your show's any good."[16]

The company got back to rehearsals and then the "costume parade" happened, where everyone, after being fitted, tried on and showed off their wonderful Raoul Pene DuBois's costumes for the production team and other cast members. It was exciting and another round of "firsts" for Meredith. Next up was the Shubert Theatre in Philadelphia, where the show would be in front of paying audiences for the first time in its life.

And the critics and Broadway sages were licking their chops and sharpening their pencils to tick the show into further oblivion.

This thing had no chance of success in their world.

Fabulous, Flubs, and Philly

Transitioning from a sleek and unencumbered gypsy run-through to an out-of-town opening complete with costumes, scenery, and a full pit orchestra is a huge step. But *The Music Man* company seemed to jump seamlessly from the Barrymore Theatre to the Shubert Theatre in Philadelphia—at least at first.

Company and crew checked into hotels. Meredith and Rini did likewise and then laid eyes on the sets for the show for the first time in the Shubert.

Meredith wrote, "We knew Howard (Bay's) sketches and designs by heart, but I must say we weren't prepared for the reality of the completed article, or the wallop and the lump that went with it."[17] The cast and crew soon jumped into initial rehearsals. Then, before they knew it, it was opening night. Then, reality set in.

Hearing the pit orchestra replace the rehearsal piano was, as usual, a jolt. The orchestrations were overall in good shape, but some sounded horrible: too loud, keys would need to be changed, and too full, overpowering the actors on stage. The 1912 period costumes (and wigs) with their petticoats, vests, buttons, and bows felt clumsy and weighty compared to the actors' rehearsal clothes they had worn throughout all their rehearsals. Plus, the theatre itself was cavernous and there were big sound problems. The audience simply could not hear everything very well. And Act One was *still* too long. "That's why we're in Philadelphia," said Meredith. "But still you sit in your seat with pounding heart and hope for a miracle."[18] But they didn't get one.

As usual, a lot of the New York theatre intelligentsia had shown up in Philadelphia as curious onlookers. At the intermission of one performance, a prominent Broadway producer who had been publicly supportive at the Barrymore run-through ignored Meredith and Rini upon seeing them. "She wore on her face the unmistakable blend of relief and superiority characteristic of any producer who has the good fortune to attend another producer's fiasco," said Meredith.[19]

He added:

> The lobby conversations I overheard were not very good and not very bad. Even at that, they liked it better than I did. Considering I had written the stuff and still couldn't hear three words out of four, I wondered why they were friendly at all. I took no notes after intermission, my tablet being already loaded down and spilling over onto my checkbook, my program, and my soul.[20]

And then, there were still other persistent Broadway wags who were predicting doom for the show who were in attendance at a few Philadelphia performances. One who had seen the Barrymore run-through and "ticked them into oblivion" was back at it: "They'll never make it," he said as he held court with his minions. "He had to come all the way from New York for the satisfaction of making that remark," added Meredith.[21]

Time for a serious production meeting. DaCosta called it. Bloomgarden was the first to speak up at the meeting, addressing the elephant in the room.

"The magic is gone," said Bloomgarden.

And they all knew it. Although the show wasn't terrible—there were no missed cues, noisy scenery, malfunctioning backdrops, wrong entrances, lighting mistakes, etc.—but still, the magic was gone. Meredith second-guessed himself: Had their imaginations supplied something at the Barrymore that didn't exist?

Finally, reviews from the local media came in. And the reviews were positive.

Meredith was ecstatic. They were home free for Broadway! Perhaps he had been too critical of his own work. But DaCosta soon brought Meredith back down to earth.

"Mere," said DaCosta. "Have you ever heard of Broadway?"

He went on:

> This is a Broadway show we have here, we hope. Regardless of how well they might like us here in Philadelphia or Washington or New Haven or London or Paris or Hong Kong or Gratz, it doesn't cut any ice.

Meredith retorted, "But the people in the theatre loved us tonight."

"Famous last words," said Bloomgarden. "So they loved us in Philadelphia. If we were going to stay here a year—great."[22] But they were not. They were heading to Broadway. Where critics and audiences are different.

In the weeks that followed, a lot was changed and improved with the show. Meredith took it on himself to investigate the sound system problems and found several microphones and a speaker that weren't working. But the opening train sequence still wasn't connecting with the audience, and that would take more than a sound system overhaul to repair.

Now known as one of the most unique openings of a Broadway musical ever, the opening train sequence, titled "Rock Island" (as in Rock Island,

Illinois, where the train originates before it stops in River City, Iowa) not only provides needed exposition—setting the stage for the period of the piece and introducing the character of Harold Hill—but it also uses spoken words to imitate the sounds of a locomotive carrying a carload of traveling salesmen. But in its iteration as seen in Philadelphia, the curtain opens, and the train is running at full steam. It was the show's company manager, Milton Pollack, who pulled Meredith aside when the production team saw from the audience's reaction that the train sequence was not working but confusing. "It should start up from idle, then get rolling up to full speed . . . then end with a hilarious jolt," Pollack suggested. Director DaCosta had the salesmen jolt, jiggle, and jump in rhythm to the train, and the result was more Broadway magic. The final icing on the cake was when Meredith suggested the orchestral accompaniment be removed and only the rhythm of the actors' speaking voices carry the entire number.

Meredith Willson (kneeling) gives Winthrop (Eddie Hodges) a cornet lesson while Robert Preston leads.
EDDIE HODGES PERSONAL COLLECTION.

One could almost say this was its own form of "rap" first heard on the Broadway stage! (This was long before the groundbreaking *Hamilton* came along.) The changes made the train opening a solid hit with Philadelphia audiences. And, according to Meredith, "That train never had to go to the roundhouse for repairs again."[23]

One more heart-stopper in Philadelphia happened when Robert Preston lost his voice during one of their final performances before embarking for New York. Preston's understudy, Larry Douglas, stepped in after the usual "put-in" run-through with the cast. Between that matinee when Preston lost his voice and the evening's performance, the cast and crew didn't leave the theatre nor eat anything. Welcome to show business. The cast and crew pulled together to help the very talented Douglas pull it off, and indeed, he did. Meanwhile, Preston had been in bed resting up for their final performances at the Shubert. He soon took the stage once again and everyone breathed a collective sigh of relief. He was ready.

Act One was shorter. The train was fixed. Champ, the live horse that pulled the Wells Fargo Wagon onto the stage at the Act One finale, knew his steps. Countless other things had been better defined and tightened. The out-of-town tryout process had served its purpose. Now it was time to see if the New York audiences and critics agreed.

Farewell, Philly.

Fifteen

THE BAND HEARD 'ROUND THE WORLD

The job of the theatre is not to feed pessimism but to dispel it.

—Morton DaCosta

Hello, New York.

It has been said that if Alexander Graham Bell had not invented the telephone, someone else would have eventually. And perhaps that's true. But as the late, great composer/conductor Marvin Hamlisch said, "Meredith Willson was the only person who could have written *The Music Man*."[1] And although the show's success seems inevitable now—even at this stage of the story— nothing could be further from the truth.

It was now December 1957, and that moment of truth was approaching. The Majestic Theatre was a welcome change from the too-large Shubert Theatre in Philadelphia. The company settled into their new theatre, and after a few run-throughs on the "new" stage—only three blocks from where they had their gypsy run-through several weeks before—they were ready for a few previews prior to opening night. One day on his way to the theatre for rehearsal, Meredith was struck with stark reality:

> I caught my breath to see a large red-and-white sign along Shubert Alley across from the Booth Theatre on Forty-Fifth Street. It was the first *Music Man* sign I'd seen in New York. I knew every crack and brick in that Shubert Alley. I took the right turn across from Sardi's, passed the Broadhurst (Theatre) with its big *Auntie Mame* signs. And there we were. Huge

blow-ups of photographed scenes from the show were all along the building. Then I saw the marquee out in front of the Majestic, our theatre. With the name there. With the two L's. Right up there.[2]

This was really happening, at long, long last. As noted, the preview performances didn't go very well—"disaster," as Meredith described their final one before opening night.[3] They realized there were still problems that needed working out. So during the preview performances, they kept at it. One of the big things that needed help was the "whispering ballet" (as Meredith called it) "Marian, the Librarian," which takes place in, of course, the library. Choreographer Onna White figured out it was crucial for Harold Hill to close the number by "bookending" it and have a final, brief, sung section as he did in the opening of the number. The change was implemented, and it landed with the final preview audience. And among those preview audiences, some of the naysayers were in full attendance. The most infamous of the lot was there, clicking his tongue in mock sympathy ticking them into final oblivion: "They shouldn't have come in," he said to his small court of admirers. "I mean they shoulda closed in Philly. Haven't got a chance."[4]

Ready or not. Naysayers or not, it was time for opening night: Thursday, December 19, 1957.

But first, as Broadway opening night traditions go, it was time for thank-you notes and gifts. From Bloomgarden:

> Dear Meredith and Rini, you have done a fine work, a glorious, happy show, and I am proud to have been associated with it. Whatever happens, meeting you and knowing you has made everything worthwhile. Love, Kermit.[5]

Rini had once told Meredith that she loved "chocolate bars from Mr. Hoover and my aunt's lorgnette." Meredith ran across one in a gift shop where he spied a gold one with small diamonds. The diamonds on one side formed a crown near the engraved letters: "B a J," which, according to the shop clerk—as told by Meredith—stood for "Bonaparte to Josephine." The other side had little diamonds forming a heart with an arrow going through: "J to L" engraved.

"Diamond Jim Brady to Lillian Russell" added the clerk. Meredith told the clerk if she could get "M to R" on it by opening night, he would buy it. "Done," said the clerk.[6] In her memoir, *Then and Now*, Barbara Cook challenges this story told by Meredith. Although acknowledging his true love for Rini, Cook adds regarding this story: "The truth is that Meredith had all of the initials added and never told Rini about it. He just wanted to please her, even if he had to fib to do it."[7]

It was showtime. Meredith and Rini were sitting in the farthest two seats over to the side under the box nearest the exit. "Plenty places to hide, easy to duck out fast," Meredith said. He had hold of her cold hand with its wet palm and she had his cold hand with its wet palm. Suddenly, the show curtain got hit with a million-candle power—and now, now, now, at long, long last, knowing positively it could never happen, pit orchestra conductor Herbert Greene raised his baton. Meredith recalled that moment vividly: "The number of things that can go through your mind that moment in a half split second reaches off into the countless, people say; adding up to a whole lifetime. As when you're drowning; or falling from a building; or waiting for the blade of a guillotine; or the downbeat of a baton. As it flashed down, I imagined I could hear that big boff laugh of [Herb's] in his apartment that cold rainy night one year ago to this day."[8]

And the rest is musical theatre history.

Time magazine described the evening in this way:

> The curtain came down that night at 11:15 p.m. EST. The pit orchestra swung into a blasting reprise of the show's biggest hit, "Seventy-Six Trombones." The audience applauds. Up goes the curtain again. And onstage for the curtain call throng the 67 men, women, boys and girls of the cast. Marching two by two they go, first to one side, then to the other, and then back again. They pantomime the players of a big brass band—trombones sliding, cornets flashing, cymbals smashing, piccolos chirping, woodwinds whining, and drumheads cracking. Abruptly, as if by some magical cue from the conductor, the 1,695 hypnotized customers in the audience begin to slam their hands together in rhythm to the march. The music wells, and the actors turn, dip, twist and prance. The applause pounds on in martial

time as, a tatatatatat, the music pours up from the pit and gilds the Majestic Theatre with shimmering sheets of brass.[9]

Cy Feuer was in the audience that night and corroborated the *Time* magazine description of the show's success with me:

> It was incredible. Simply electric. The curtain kept going up and down and up and down for the standing ovation the cast received. And afterwards, Ernie and I licked our wounds on how we'd really missed it . . . we had *The Music Man* in our grip and foolishly let it go. I had even given Meredith the title of the show. Ernie and I always regretted that one that got away.[10]

The critics were effusive and giddy. From the *New York Times* proclamation that the show was "As American as apple pie and a Fourth of July oration" to *Time* magazine calling it "one of the happiest chemical explosions to hit the street since John Philip Sousa himself marched grandly into town," the superlatives flowed abundantly and freely.

Feuer went backstage afterward, and it was "mayhem," he recalled. "Everyone was in total elation . . . knowing that their lives would never be the same. They were in a hit Broadway musical."

After Bloomgarden had to raise the money for the show piecemeal because there weren't a lot of big-time backers who believed in what they thought was "Iowa corn," the musical paid investors back ten to one. And that was just the Broadway production, let alone its future iterations.

The naysayers were now nowhere to be found.

After that explosive opening night, the good vibrations would be coming for decades literally around the world.

The musical won five Tony Awards, including Best Musical, winning in the same year that *West Side Story* was also nominated for the award. Preston, Cook, and Burns also won. Liza Redfield became the first woman to be the full-time conductor of a Broadway pit orchestra when she assumed the role of music director for the original production's final year of performances.

The Music Man *theatrical poster.*
PUBLIC DOMAIN.

Another Op'nin' and Other Shows

The long-running U.S. national tour of the show opened in 1958, starring For-rest Tucker as Hill and Joan Weldon as Marian. The first Australian production in Melbourne opened in March 1960, followed by another Australian produc-tion in Sydney later that year. The first production in the United Kingdom opened in 1961 at the Bristol Hippodrome, later transferring to the West End's Adelphi Theatre. Then, a two-week revival at New York City Centre ran in June 1965 with Bert Parks as Hill. A three-week revival, directed and choreographed by top-notch choreographer Michael Kidd ran in June 1980 that featured Dick Van Dyke as Hill and Christian Slater as Winthrop. In 1987, a Chinese translation of the musical was staged at Beijing's Central Opera Theatre. Rosemary Willson remembered the Chinese production vividly:

> I was fortunate enough to be in Beijing for the production, and it was so thrilling, because the music is universal. They had a production crew from the United States go over and work with the Chinese performers. Once the performance started, everything fell into place and I could understand everything, even in a different language. The laughs came in the same places! The "Shipoopi" number went over big.[11]

A New York City Opera–staged revival happened in February to April 1988. And then, in April of 2000, *The Music Man* officially returned to Broadway for the first open-ended run since its original production. Directed and choreographed by Susan Stroman, with Craig Bierko and Rebecca Luker in the lead roles, the production ran for a healthy 699 performances.

On the screen, the Warner Brothers film version of the show was released in 1962 starring Robert Preston and Shirley Jones in the lead roles. In 2003, fueled by the success of the 2000 revival, a television film version was produced for ABC-TV with Matthew Broderick and Kristin Chenoweth mixing it up as Hill and Marian. Keep reading for more details on these film versions in the next chapter.

Another Broadway revival opened in February 2022 at the Winter Garden Theatre starring Hugh Jackman and Sutton Foster in the lead roles. Other Broadway veterans Shuler Hensley, Jefferson Mays, and Jane Houdyshell completed the cast. The production, directed by Jerry Zaks with choreography by Warren Carlyle, also included a stellar lineup of top-notch producers. Most reviews were extremely positive, showing that this show has no signs of slowing down.

And There Was Music

The first recording of "Till There Was You" was released before the original cast album version. Promotional copies of the 45 RPM single were released on November 26, 1957, even before the original production had opened. Performed by Nelson Riddle and his orchestra, the recording helped create an early buzz about the show.

As previously noted, the original cast recording was released by Capitol Records on January 20, 1958, and held the number-one spot on the Billboard charts for 12 weeks, remaining on the charts for a total of 245 weeks. The album was awarded "Best Original Cast Album" at the first-ever Grammy Awards ceremony in 1958 and was inducted in 1998 as a Grammy Hall of Fame Award winner.

"Till There Was You" was recorded by numerous artists after the Broadway opening of the show, but the most famous recording of the song was from the Beatles on their second LP *With the Beatles* (issued as *Meet the Beatles* in the United States). Rosemary Willson told me the revenues from the Beatles' recording of this song generated more royalties than did the entire run of the original Broadway production.

Pop Goes the Show

The Music Man has found its way into popular culture numerous times. It was parodied on *The Simpsons* episode, "Marge vs. the Monorail," written by Conan O'Brien, who is an avowed fan of the show. O'Brien also sang a parody version of "Ya Got Trouble" in his opening monologue of the 2006 Emmy Awards broadcast.

The television program *Family Guy* has parodied the musical at least three times because *Family Guy*'s creator, Seth McFarland, is another big fan of the show. Other TV shows that have referenced or parodied the show include *Boston Legal*, *Ally McBeal*, *My Little Pony*, and a Netflix original show *Grace and Frankie*.

With the reverberations of the success this show heard on that opening night in 1957, chatter soon started about a film version. Although the movie adaptation wouldn't hit the screen until 1962, when it did, it created another successful parade.

Sixteen

LIGHTS, CAMERA, HOLLYWOOD!

> Movies will make you famous; television will make you rich; but theatre
> will make you good.
>
> —Terrence Mann

Film adaptations of Broadway musicals have a mixed record of success, to say the least. Transitioning a musical from the stage to the different medium of film can bring even bigger success for the piece than it enjoyed on Broadway (*The Sound of Music*) or result in disappointment (*South Pacific*). Nevertheless, Hollywood, especially during the Broadway musical's golden age, could never resist the possibility of a commercially if not also critically successful film version of a hit show. And *The Music Man* was certainly no exception.

Seventeen months into the Broadway run of the show, Meredith wrote a letter to his agent, Julius Lefkowitz:

> He who does not note the falling leaf can also overlook the fact that the winter is not far behind. For the first time since *Music Man* opened we missed capacity two weeks in a row. A very small leaf, true, but a leaf none-theless. I would appreciate it if the timetable could be moved up a little with respect to readying a draft of the movie deal on paper.[1]

Although Meredith's show was still going strong on Broadway, the inevitable slowdown of ticket sales was just barely beginning to appear, but it appeared nevertheless. And he wasn't about to let his show be seen as a less-than-desirable property in Hollywood. So Lefkowitz got busy and the "usual suspects" of the film industry (MGM, Warner Bros., 20th Century Fox) were lined up and negotiations began.

Not to be outbid, Jack Warner at Warner Brothers stepped up and offered a healthy $1 million for the screen rights to the show. And that was that. Deal closed.

Warner was wise to then enlist director Morton DaCosta of the original Broadway version to direct the film. Having the director of the original show also direct the film version was a rarity, however, but that decision paid off handsomely for Warner Bros. DaCosta was also given the role of producer for the film, expanding his creative control over what went on film. This was another smart move on Warner's part, to ensure the spirit and style of the original stage production that made it such a hit translated to the screen.

Onna White, another *Music Man* Broadway production original, was signed to re-create and expand her original choreography. Others enlisted to create what has now become a film classic were Dorothy Jeakins to create the sumptuous 1912 costumes; Paul Grosse, one of MGM's leading art directors, to design the eighteen-plus sets used in the picture; and Warner Bros. music department head, veteran Ray Heindorf, as music director and conductor of the fifty-five-piece studio orchestra. Successful screenwriter Marion Hargrove was contracted to write the screenplay. So the production team was solid, anchored by those who made the show a hit on Broadway.

Next came casting. A wrong step in this area could sink the efforts of even the best production team. It was déjà vu for Meredith when names were tossed around as to who would—and could—play Harold Hill for the film version. Cary Grant? Frank Sinatra? Gene Kelly? Bing Crosby? Meredith put his foot down: Without Robert Preston in the titular role, there would be no film version of *The Music Man*. Rosemary Willson remembered Meredith's emphatic stance on this based on what he told her years afterward:

> Meredith was unbending on the casting of Bob Preston in the role of Harold Hill for the film version of the show. Warner Bros. thought that Frank Sinatra would have tremendous box office appeal but having seen Bob create the role on Broadway and give an opening night performance every night, Meredith knew Bob owned the role. Frank ran into Meredith

at a party when it was announced the film would be made and Frank said something to the effect "When do we begin filming, Meredith?" and was dead serious. Tec [DaCosta] agreed with Meredith. Bob Preston was the man for the film. Period.[2]

Fortunately, for Preston—and everyone who agrees that he was the inevitable choice—Meredith's insistence paid off, and Preston's immortal performance as Harold Hill is forever preserved on film for all to see and enjoy. Next came Marian Paroo.

Doris Day was a name bandied about early on as a possibility, but that idea eventually fell apart for various reasons. The original creator of the role, Barbara Cook, was naturally considered, at least by DaCosta. And although Cook had a loyal following and critical acclaim in New York theatre circles, with no film roles to her credit, the role could not be hers on film. In a letter to Meredith dated July 11, 1960, DaCosta recommended Shirley MacLaine, Shirley Jones, and Mitzi Gaynor as Marian.[3] Although both MacLaine and Gaynor clearly had theatre "chops," and movie box office draw as well to their credit, it was Jones who won the role. After all, she had been Rodgers and Hammerstein's pick as the ingenue in the film adaptations of two of their most successful stage properties: *Oklahoma!* (Laurey) and *Carousel* (Julie). Plus, she was fresh off her Academy Award–winning performance in the film adaptation of the best-selling Sinclair Lewis novel *Elmer Gantry*.

Other principal roles fell nicely into place with some being filled by original Broadway cast members: veteran stage and television actor Pert Kelton as Mrs. Paroo and the Buffalo Bills as the barbershop quartet. Shirley Jones recalled "[Pert] was just great. She originated the role of Mrs. Paroo on Broadway. She had been in the business forever, and she was a consummate professional. She knew every little nuance of that part."[4]

Other roles were filled with actors from the show's national touring production or as Broadway replacements: Paul Ford as Mayor Shinn and Susan Luckey as Zaneeta, for example. Finally, rounding out the cast in key roles included seasoned performers Hermoine Gingold as Eulalie Mackechnie Shinn; comedian Buddy Hackett as Marcellus Washburn; Timmy Everett as

Tommy Djilas, and young Ron Howard as Winthrop, who had just completed his first season as Opie on *The Andy Griffith Show*.

"Our company was top-notch in every detail, and I count myself lucky to have been in their numbers," Shirley said of the cast.[5]

There was some preproduction talk by DaCosta about building the exterior set of River City streets and buildings somewhere in Iowa to give it more authenticity—and then use the sets as a visitor attraction after filming was completed. But the impracticality of that idea soon caused it to be scrapped, and River City was born on the Warner Bros. backlot and soundstages, where a complete River City was built on three acres. It's interesting and slightly comical to see basically flat Mason City (River City) depicted with the beautiful Hollywood hills in the background. Ironically, there now is a reproduction of the main street of *The Music Man* film ensconced in Mason City at the Music Man Square (more on it later) museum.

With casting completed, now it was time to get to work.

The film began shooting on April 3, 1961. Seven weeks prior, rehearsals had commenced on the dance numbers with the soundtrack being recorded in the studio for playback and lip sync during shooting. Once, I had the pleasure of meeting Shirley Jones in her Los Angeles home to visit with her about some possible fundraising efforts for The Music Man Square and other potential projects. I asked her about the process of prerecording the soundtrack for the musical films in which she had appeared. I was always curious if the soloists in the film were given tapes of those recordings to then take home and rehearse with on their own so their lip syncing would be tight on the day of shooting and not "rubbery" as it's sometimes called when the singer's mouth movements don't quite match the recording on screen. She confirmed that indeed, that is the case (which made sense to me). Anyone who has seen Shirley's performance in the film during her musical solos can see that she did her homework. Her lip syncing is flawless. The same can be said of Robert Preston, especially when he's lip syncing the complex and super rapid-fire "Ya Got Trouble." An amazing feat.

Warner Bros. Records released the film's soundtrack simultaneously with the release of the film. Jones said in her promotion of the recording at its release regarding its production process, "I must say I've never seen a composer dance around a studio before, and that's just what Meredith Willson did after first hearing the playbacks of [the soundtrack for] *The Music Man*."[6]

Jones remembered, "The first time I met [choreographer] Onna [White], I told her, 'I've got to tell you, I'm a klutz. I'm not a dancer.' And she said, 'Honey, by the time this movie's over, you'll be a dancer!' We had a good time, and I said, 'Ok, it's up to you.' She was a marvelous choreographer. And patient."[7]

"Shipoopi" is the biggest dance number in the film. The song features the hilarious Buddy Hackett. The word "Shipoopi" has no actual meaning other than being created by Meredith to describe a desirable sort of sweetheart.

In his book, *The Boys*, cowritten with his brother Clint Howard, Ron tells a behind-the-scenes story of his inability to nail the choreography given to him by White in the song "Gary, Indiana." At the end of the song, his character Winthrop—with his newfound confidence and exuberance, thanks to Harold Hill—breaks into a short dance routine:

> I got no rhythm. [I practiced the steps in tap shoes but] wasn't going to be wearing [them] in the movie, but this way I could hear my steps as I took them, which provided confirmation of whether I was on or off the beat. We thought we had the routine down, but before we shot the scene, Morton DaCosta asked us to do a rehearsal run. Despite [Onna White and coach Mrs. Webber]'s gentle encouragement, I kept messing up. After a couple of tries, I heard DaCosta sigh and tell the camera operator, "Dolly in and cut him at the knees." Having weathered a season of series television, I knew not to be alarmed by such a turn of a phrase. DaCosta only meant that they were going to frame out my feet. With a hint of exasperation, he told me, "Just turn around in a circle at the end, and we'll put the steps in with sound."[8]

So thanks to DaCosta's quick thinking—and the Warner Bros. sound effects person—Ron as Winthrop appears to totally crush it in the dance area as a child hoofer—movie magic.

Shirley Jones reminisced about working with Ron Howard on the film:

> Ronnie Howard was a gem of a little boy and a gem of an actor. He was very unusual. A real old soul. And of course, he's a very active member of

the movie community now. But he was an incredible actor. I never saw a young person that had the intelligence and the foresight of everything he was doing. He came from a wonderful family and was not a "show-biz kid." He was just a little boy. But brilliant.[9]

During the nine-week shoot, the cast became much like a big family, celebrating birthdays and other special occasions with cake. "We ate a lot of birthday cake during those nine weeks," Jones remembered. And although eating a lot of birthday cake could have been a concern for some cast members about putting on weight, Shirley had her own concerns about picking up several pounds during filming. She became pregnant.

Unsure as to how to handle it, Shirley asked for a lunch meeting with DaCosta. And while he shared Shirley's joy about her news, DaCosta knew others in the production company would become nervous that the film wouldn't be completed now that she was with child. "Nobody must know . . . nobody," warned DaCosta. "We'll wrap you in sashes and bows as you show more and more," he added. But, Shirley said, Robert Preston eventually found out about the pregnancy accidentally.

"It was finale day, and we were shooting the magical footbridge scene where Professor Harold Hill [Preston] and Marian the Librarian finally embrace and kiss and sing their way into a glorious Happy Ever After," Shirley recalled.

"At this point, I was standing on the footbridge, looking at Harold Hill and ready to sing 'Till There Was You.' It's the third take . . . the music begins, Preston reaches out for me and pulls me close . . . very close . . . begins to speak . . . and sing . . . when suddenly . . . BOOM . . . Bob LEAPS back a giant three-foot leap . . . piercing the humongous soundstage with his great, round baritone: 'What the hell was that???'"

Shirley continued, "The music stopped. Nobody moved, nobody spoke, everybody waiting for the Earth to open somewhere and save the day for all of us."

Finally, Meredith Willson spoke from the back of the giant soundstage, breaking the silence, his words resonating as if they were spoken from the Grand Canyon: "That, Mister Preston, was Patrick William Cassidy."

Shirley said the laughter started slowly, then grew to envelop everybody.

"I guess it was very much in keeping with the joy on *The Music Man* set that reflected Meredith Willson's labor of love to the very last shot on the very last day."[10]

Fast-forward around twenty-two years later, when the all-grown-up Patrick Cassidy was attending a Broadway show that starred Robert Preston. Of course, Patrick had heard all his life the story of him startling Preston from his mother's stomach once upon a time. Cassidy couldn't wait to meet Preston at last, so he went backstage after the show. After being ushered into Preston's dressing room, he said, "Mr. Preston, I'm Patrick Cassidy."

Without missing a beat, Preston responded, "I know. We've already met."[11]

All of the show's songs were retained in their full versions for the film, with some exceptions: "Rock Island" was slightly edited; the middle verse of "My White Knight" was retained but the remainder of the song was replaced with "Being in Love" with new music and lyrics by Meredith. Another change from the stage version is when Harold Hill runs into his old friend Marcellus where the latter now works in a livery stable, who reveals Hill's actual name is "Gregory." So Harold Hill is obviously an alias name to help him keep slipping away from justice in his schemes.

Morton DaCosta brought an inventive bit of camerawork to the film, which he first used effectively in the film version of *Auntie Mame*, that he had also directed. The "iris-in" and "iris-out" effect isolates a character, giving the character depth and focus as previously only done in a close-up. When watching *The Music Man* film, one can easily spot this creative technique when the background dissolves to black behind the character(s) in the scene, leaving only the character(s) silhouetted against a black background for a moment before dissolving to the next scene.

For the closing final parade scene featuring the hit song "Seventy-Six Trombones," Jack Warner selected the University of Southern California's marching band, The Spirit of Troy, to join the full cast. Many junior high school students from Southern California were also included, forming most the band. It took approximately eight hours of shooting over two days to film the approximately three-minute sequence. All the musical instruments used for the production were custom-made for the film by the Olds Instrument Company of Fullerton, California. The instruments were then refurbished after the production wrapped and sold as "slightly used," with no indication they were ever used in the film.

After principal photography was completed in mid-July, the team at Pacific Title in California got to work and tackled the snail's pace process of stop-animation filming for the creation of one of the most creative title sequences in a Hollywood film: a miniature animated marching band forming the title and key credit words and names.

After the film's final edit, it was ready for a world premiere. Perhaps in New York City, where the show was born on Broadway? Or Grauman's Chinese Theatre, where countless films were premiered in those days, with all the glitz and glamour that accompanies a flashy Hollywood premiere.

No, once again, Meredith and his *Music Man* played against type. The film premiered on June 19, 1962, in Mason City, Iowa . . . where *The Music Man* was really born.

The Music Man *original film poster.*
PUBLIC DOMAIN.

The film was given a special press premiere at Mason City's Palace Theater, in conjunction with the annual North Iowa Band Festival, which was highlighted by a marching band contest among one hundred different schools. Warner Bros. added substantially to the festival's modest annual budget to lift the event to the stratosphere. Attendance at the festival grew to a staggering 100,000 people that year due to the premiere of the film. The national press were in full attendance. Also in attendance: Meredith and Rini Willson, of course, along with Morton DaCosta, Robert Preston, Shirley Jones, Ron Howard, The Buffalo Bills Quartet, plus state and local dignitaries. The usual two-day event was expanded to three, and in addition to the film's premiere, it was packed with marching bands, picnics, cast meet-and-greets, and of course a grand parade. At one moment in the parade while Meredith and Rini were coming down the street sitting on the back seats of an open convertible, Meredith jumped out and grabbed the baton from the Mason City High School Band drum major who was leading the band (playing "Seventy-Six Trombones" at that moment) behind Meredith and Rini's car. Meredith proceeded to lead the band for several blocks while the locals ate it up. A picture was snapped of the moment Meredith "led the big parade."

"The premiere weekend was an extraordinary event," remembered Shirley, "and our Iowa hosts treated us like family."[12] Legendary Hollywood gossip columnist Hedda Hopper covered the event, and in her report on the occasion, she described the premiere itself:

> It was 11:00 p.m. before the world premiere of *The Music Man* got underway at the theatre. But it went beautifully. At the finish when they played "Seventy-Six Trombones," the roof literally fell in . . . a perfect climax for a perfect day.[13]

Meredith was overwhelmed. "If I stood a little straighter and a little taller than my years might normally permit," he said, "it was chiefly because I'm from Mason City, Iowa."[14]

Once again, Meredith's tour de force of a show—now a film "on one of those giant, Technicolor, eighty-seven dimensional stereo screens," according to Meredith—was showered with critical and box office success. Bosley Crowther in the *New York Times* wrote:

Robert Preston and Shirley Jones in The Music Man.
PHOTO COURTESY MEREDITH WILLSON PAPERS, GREAT AMERICAN SONGBOOK FOUNDATION.

It's here, and the rich, ripe roundness of it, the lush amalgam of the many elements of successful American show business that Mr. Willson brought together on the stage, has been preserved and appropriately made rounder and richer through the magnitude of the film.[15]

A few weeks later, the film had subsequent openings in major cities around the United States and then was released to smaller markets across the nation. Reception for the film was ecstatic, and it enjoyed high praise and high box office receipts. *The Music Man* became the third highest-grossing film of 1962. It garnered six Academy Award nominations, including one for Best Picture (losing to *Lawrence of Arabia*). It captured the statue for Best Musical Score.

In 2005, *The Music Man* was selected for preservation in the U.S. National Film Registry by the Library of Congress as being "culturally, historically, or aesthetically significant."[16]

Shirley Jones shared her thoughts about what made the film and story a success:

I really do believe Meredith Willson believed in the innate goodness of all mankind. He saw the good in everyone. Even a con man named Harold Hill. What Meredith is telling us, is that in the magic of believing in the goodness of life, miracles do happen. Even for a skeptic like Marian Paroo. *The Music Man* is a miraculous work, and I'm honored to have been a part of bringing it to the screen. The magic of believing is powerful stuff. If you concentrate hard enough, you just might hear those seventy-six trombones.[17]

With a Capital "B" and That Stands for "Broderick"

On February 16, 2003 . . . almost forty-one years to the month that Warner Bros.' *Music Man* film premiered, ABC-TV premiered a television film version of the show. Produced by the highly respected team of Craig Zadan and Neil Meron, and directed by Jeff Bleckner with a teleplay by Sally Robinson, it starred Matthew Broderick in the title role. Other principal cast members included Kristin Chenoweth (Marian); David Aaron Baker (Marcellus); Debra Monk (Mrs. Paroo); Victor Garber (Mayor Shinn); and Molly Shannon (Eulalie Mackechnie Shinn). It was broadcast as part of *The Wonderful World of Disney* and seen by 13.1 million viewers.

Most reviewers found the film inferior to the 1962 version, and Broderick's performance as Hill was generally compared unfavorably to Robert Preston's. Edward Guthmann of the *San Francisco Chronicle* called it "passable entertainment" with "strong production values, excellent costumes and art direction, and a rich color palette that conjures cozy notions of small-town America in the early 20th century." Kathleen Marshall choreographed and received some good notices. The production was nominated for five Emmy Awards, including Outstanding Choreography and Music Direction and Outstanding Art Direction, Costumes, and Single Camera Sound Mixing for a Miniseries or a Movie. Director Jeff Bleckner was nominated for a Directors Guild of America Award for Outstanding Directing—Television Film but lost to Mike Nichols for *Angels in America*.

But mixed reviews aside for this television film version, *13.1 million viewers were exposed to the property*—many of whom were likely younger viewers seeing the piece for the first time. To put the power of this prime-time television presentation into perspective, it would take almost eight thousand performances—running for nineteen years—of the show at the Majestic Theatre on Broadway (*The Music Man*'s original stage production's home) to be seen by that many people. The show's original Broadway run was for 1,375 performances—running over three years. Clearly, the ABC-TV *Wonderful World of Disney* version had an impact of introducing the show to new customers and a new generation . . . let alone that of the genre of musical theatre. Had Meredith been alive when this version was released, he would probably (or most certainly) have been partial to the DaCosta original film version, but he would inevitably have been pleased with many aspects of it, especially the wide exposure and big numbers his "baby" achieved that broadcast night, in subsequent airings, and in its home video release.

The Music Man still had legs.

Seventeen

MOLLY BROWN AIN'T DOWN YET

As long as they're talking about me, I don't care what they say.

—Margaret Tobin "Molly" Brown

Once a creator of a hit Broadway show has breathed that rarified air, with its box office bonanza, triumphant opening night reviews, and standing ovations—to say nothing of the financial rewards—it's understandable that they would want to do it all again. And again. And if possible . . . AGAIN! When you get down to it, only a limited number of composers in the Broadway universe have ever enjoyed habitual and hit commercial successes, with critical acclaim coupled with it. Rodgers and Hammerstein, Stephen Sondheim, Andrew Lloyd Webber, Charles Strouse, Cy Coleman, and Stephen Schwartz to name several. But the list certainly isn't endless.

With the incredible success of *The Music Man* on Broadway, Meredith became one of the hottest properties in the New York theatre scene at that time. And the offers to write his next musical were flowing freely. But the great Richard Rodgers, quite taken with the seemingly out-of-nowhere and surprising success of Meredith and his *Music Man*, invited Meredith to lunch at the famous Sardi's.

Meredith recalled what Rodgers told him soon after sitting down: "I'll tell you right off the bat why I asked you here," said Rodgers. "As you know, I'm a tremendous fan in the same profession with you." Meredith replied, "That's the finest compliment I've ever received." Rodgers continued, "Now for the advice: Everyone will be coming to you with a property. I beg you not to do another show until you are as possessed with it as you were with the first."[1]

In those euphoric days that followed the opening of *The Music Man*, Willson told an interviewer that between eighty and one hundred potential musical properties came his way, virtually anything to do with the American past. He rejected the idea of a musical version of Edna Ferber's novel *Saratoga Trunk*, material he couldn't relate to. Harold Arlen and Johnny Mercer would write that score, and the show, called *Saratoga*—with a libretto and direction by Morton DaCosta—would come and quickly go in 1959 after only eighty performances. Willson was apparently also offered what became *Take Me Along*, a musical version of Eugene O'Neill's nostalgic comedy *Ah, Wilderness!* He passed on it because he felt he would just be repeating himself. Bob Merrill wrote the score and *Take Me Along* was a moderate success (448 performances) the same season *Saratoga* flopped. Some other properties tempted him, but as Willson said, none "enchanted" him.[2]

It was Meredith's trusted friend and colleague Morton DaCosta who, in 1959, read a musical libretto by Richard Morris for a show called *The Unsinkable Mrs. Brown*, to be directed by playwright, director, and producer Dore Schary and coproduced by him with the Theatre Guild. DaCosta recommended Schary send the libretto to Willson, who read it, quickly identified with the subject, and concluded that he simply liked the two leading female and male characters . . . that being the most crucial point for him connecting with the property. And one can see how Meredith might have been drawn, if only subconsciously, to the new characters: The leads for *Molly Brown* were somewhat opposites, yet similar of those from *The Music Man*. In *Music Man*, the charismatic male lead (Harold Hill) is primarily a "speak-singer" and the ingenue female lead (Marian) needs a beautiful solo voice. In *Molly*, the role types are similar but reversed: The female lead (Molly) is the charismatic lead and the male ingenue (Johnny) needs the beautiful solo voice.

"If you'll take the cussin' out of there and be mindful of the beautifying of the love story, I'm your boy," Willson told Schary and Morris.[3]

Schary described his involvement in the musical:

> Want to do a musical? Lend me your ears. The principal reason I wanted to was that I'd never done one. It was that simple. And that's the last time I'll use the word "simple" in connection with a musical. Putting one together

is slightly less complicated than assembling a nuclear reactor, but I discovered that the explosive potential is just about as great. However, in the long run, it's probably more fun. Shattering, but fun.[4]

Richard Morris was born in Burlingame, California, and attended the Chouinard Art Institute in Los Angeles before services in the Army during World War II. After the war, he studied acting under Sanford Meisner, while writing sketch comedy for fledgling performers such as Kay Ballard. His work was eventually noticed by a talent scout from Universal Studios, which led to Morris writing screenplays for *Finders Keepers* (1951) and *Ma and Pa Kettle at the Fair* (1952). In the mid-1950s, he started writing for television, and in 1955 became the head writer/director of NBC-TV's *The Loretta Young Show*, for which he received an Emmy nomination.

Morris first became aware of Molly Brown in 1955 when he visited Central City, a picturesque hamlet outside Denver. Here he was introduced to the legend of the illiterate girl from Hannibal, Missouri, who married Leadville Johnny Brown, a gangling Irish prospector who found the richest silver mine in Colorado. He dreamed of seeing the story dramatized on stage.

By 1957, Morris had fully formulated his hope and plans for what he called *The Unsinkable Mrs. Brown*. But no composer or lyricist had become attached to the project. The project continued to knock around for a few more years, eventually being produced as a television presentation (with no music) as a part of an anthology series, with Cloris Leachman playing the title role. But when Meredith became attached to the property in 1959, things started to happen with an eye toward a new musical comedy on Broadway.

One of the first changes after Meredith got on board with the project was to fine-tune the title from *The Unsinkable Mrs. Brown* to *The Unsinkable Molly Brown*. Meredith wrote of his feelings on traveling the road to Broadway once again:

> Back to the hinterlands and the excitement and nervousness of a pre-Broadway opening. Back to the first thrilling look at the new scenery stacked up on the stage at the Shubert Theatre in Philadelphia; the first hanging of the show curtain. Back to another heart-in-the-throat [out-of-town] opening night and the subsequent month of alternately changing

and rehearsing, changing and rehearsing, changing and rehearsing. Back to endless pacings in the lobby. Back to the re-writes in the ladies' toilet, the re-orchestrating; noisy new sets for the crew; stiff, unfamiliar new shoes for the dancers; hot heavy hanks of hair for the singers. The first look at the theatre marquee is always a little jab in the solar plexus.[5]

So Meredith was fully aware this time of what he was in for. And yet, he said "Yes!" That rarified air is hard not to want to breathe once more. And Schary longed to breathe it for the first time.

Most, if not all, readers of this book are likely familiar with the plot of *The Music Man*, though some may not be as familiar with the plot of *The Unsinkable Molly Brown*. So a brief summary is probably in order at this point:

Early in the twentieth century, feisty and illiterate tomboy Molly Tobin wrestles with her three younger brothers and tells them and her father that she wants to learn to read and write and find a rich husband. Molly makes her way to the Saddle Rock Saloon in Leadville, Colorado, and applies for a job. On the way to Leadville, she meets J. J. "Leadville" Johnny Brown, who falls in love with her and promises to give her whatever she wants in life. After they marry, Johnny sells a claim and provides Molly with the money she wants, enough to enter the high social life in Denver. Molly and Johnny, now dressed in gaudy finery, are made fun of by the Denver society elite she wanted to impress. Molly and Johnny then travel to Europe to "up their game" culturally, against Johnny's better instincts. The couple, especially Molly, are welcomed and accepted by European royalty, but the romantic intentions of Prince DeLong toward Molly upset Johnny and he returns to Leadville alone. Molly realizes that Johnny is her true love, and she sails home on the RMS *Titanic*. As the *Titanic* sinks and the tragedy unfolds, Molly survives in one of the lifeboats. She is finally reunited with Johnny, who has built Molly her own "castle," a beautiful home in the Rocky Mountains.

The plot of *Molly Brown* was based on the real person of Margaret Tobin Brown, and her actual survival as a passenger on the *Titanic*. However, Richard Morris's book took much creative license in Molly's story, which would not be told more authentically on the stage until a revival of the show came decades later (details on that revival to come).

The Music Man's tough slog to Broadway was clearly known in theatre circles, and accordingly its big success caught Broadway by surprise. Capitol Records, which had made the original cast recording for *The Music Man*—a recording that no other record companies seemed to want before the show opened—would realize some $6 million in profits from the best-selling *Music Man* album by the time Meredith announced he was ready to write another show. It was no surprise, then, that Capitol wanted a bigger piece of the action this time. Mindful of the profits Columbia Records shared with its investment in *My Fair Lady*, the company announced in May of 1960 that it would invest $220,000 in *The Unsinkable Molly Brown*, almost half of the show's budget, and would also make the original cast recording.[6]

With the financing coming much easier this time, and at a much faster pace than it had for Meredith's first Broadway outing, the show needed a star, a truly larger-than-life "unsinkable" Molly Brown. All manner of performers, from Lisa Kirk to Shelley Winters, auditioned for the title role, and Shirley MacLaine's name was loudly ballyhooed in the trade papers as a possible Molly. But Meredith—who had helped make a theatrical legend out of a man whom many thought was nothing but a washed-up, third-rank movie actor named Robert Preston—had his eyes open and receptive to another true talent that was a perfect fit for this material. He happened on that talent at an audition where he heard a young woman sing "Melancholy Baby" in her own unique whiskey-voiced tone. That singer/actress was Tammy Grimes.[7]

Rini Willson gets the credit for discovering Harve Presnell, who was a strapping young baritone when he first came to Rini and Meredith's attention. They were attending an evening of the music of Rodgers and Hammerstein at the famed Hollywood Bowl, where he was a featured soloist. There was nothing on Meredith's radar for Presnell at that moment, but when Molly Brown came along, Rini and Meredith had not forgotten him nor his impressive voice. He got the call and the role of "Leadville" Johnny Brown. And Presnell had not even seen a Broadway musical before being cast in one.

An interesting footnote to Presnell's career: His stage experience in *Molly Brown* led to film roles, which then waned as he aged. However, in his early sixties, he saw a resurgence in his movie career, which lasted until his death. He played character roles in films such as *Fargo* (1996), *Saving Private Ryan*

(1998), and *Flags of Our Fathers* (2006). He also appeared on television in *The Pretender, The New Adventures of Superman*, and *Dawson's Creek*.

The Trek to Opening Night

Meredith got busy writing the new score, spending more than a year on it. He enjoyed describing his creative process to interviewers: long strolls around his California home, which often yielded bits of lyrics, musical motives, and sometimes entire songs, followed by a work session that usually began with writing the words first. Johnny Brown's soaring love song "I'll Never Say No" came to him while swimming at the Palm Springs home of Glen Wallach, then head of Capitol Records. The score he created was clearly in his own inimitable style, yet uniquely fashioned to tell the story of Molly Brown. He wrote a "Seventy-Six Trombones"–styled march titled "I Ain't Down Yet" as the opening song (reprised later in the show). And as he had done with *The Music Man*, Meredith again made use of clever internal musical references in his score. For example, when illiterate and dirt-poor Molly wistfully dreams of a red silk dress at one point in the song "I Ain't Down Yet," a snippet of that melody doubles as the same melody Prince DeLong sings to her in Act Two in the beautiful ballad, "Dolce Far Niente." And there's a rousing solo with chorus echoes in an almost "Ya Got Trouble" style that Molly sings to the people of Denver. Instead of warning of the dangers of a pool table, she's selling the citizens on the idea of giving money to a local church ("Are You Sure?").

With score and script readied for the first rehearsal, on the morning of Monday, August 29, 1960, director Schary assembled the cast at the Ambassador Theatre in New York City. With the production team and crew watching, *The Unsinkable Molly Brown* came to life for the first time in the read-through. Also on board as choreographer was a young Peter Gennaro, who had assisted Jerome Robbins with his breakthrough work on *West Side Story*. Gennaro was fresh off his choreographic work for *Fiorello!* Nearly twenty years later, he would go on to choreograph the original production of *Annie*, as well as a 1997 revival of the work. After a few weeks of intense rehearsals in New York, just as with *The Music Man*, the show was ready for its first "gypsy" run-through. Expectations for the show were high: Lawrence Langner of The Theatre Guild said after the first run-through that he hadn't heard anything so good since the Guild produced the landmark hit *Oklahoma!*[8] High praise, indeed, and the show would have a lot to live up to if it were to equal or cross that bar.

Next, it was on to Philadelphia and the Shubert Theatre for a five-week run to work out the kinks. Songs were added, subtracted; dialogue overhauled in places, etc. All the usual birthing pains a show experiences in its run up to a Broadway opening. And on September 26, 1960, the show received its world premiere. But nothing is easy: Tammy Grimes lost her voice during the first week of shows and missed six performances during the tryout period. But truly proving herself as "unsinkable," she was back in fine form soon to complete the preview period. Reviews, although positive, acknowledged there was still work to be done during the five-week run in Philly before the show opened on Broadway. And unlike the negative word of mouth *The Music Man* had received from some naysayers prior to its Broadway opening, *The Unsinkable Molly Brown* had positive word of mouth about the show.

The show transferred from Philadelphia to New York City and Broadway for its opening on November 30, 1960, at the Winter Garden Theatre (right up Broadway, where the original production of *The Music Man* was still playing and also the home of the 2022 revival of *The Music Man*). Conductor Herbert Greene, as he had with *The Music Man*, gave the downbeat for the orchestra

Tammy Grimes and Harve Presnell in The Unsinkable Molly Brown.
PHOTO COURTESY MEREDITH WILLSON PAPERS, GREAT AMERICAN SONGBOOK FOUNDATION.

once again. Meredith knew his show's musical tempos and pace were literally in good hands.

The reviews came in after that auspicious opening night: Although Grimes received rave reviews, notices for the show itself were mixed. Meredith was basically up against himself (i.e., *The Music Man*) just as Lerner and Loewe were with their next big show after *My Fair Lady*. *Camelot* opened on Broadway exactly one month following *Molly Brown*'s Broadway opening. The critics' unanimous opinion regarding *Camelot* was "it's no *My Fair Lady*," and the critics felt likewise with Molly Brown: "It's no *Music Man*." Unfair? Yes, probably. But inevitable, nevertheless.

"'Unsinkable Molly' Fails to Float" read the headline in the *New York Mirror*. Of the seven daily critics, only two filed positive reviews. Most of the blame for the show's failings was laid on the script, but some earlier complaints about Meredith's tuneful score being a bit too "frenetic" lingered.[9]

But unsinkable Meredith and his show weren't down yet. In an unprecedented move, Meredith, Morris, and Schary issued a joint press release stating that they wouldn't enter into any discussion of the critics or their reviews. The three emphasized the popular reaction of the audiences who'd seen the show, and they praised the cast. Besides, with healthy advanced ticket sales and heavy prebooking with group ticket sales, plus Tammy Grimes's star turn as Molly, this show seemed to have a chance to truly stay afloat.

And stay afloat it did . . . for 532 performances, closing on February 10, 1962. Not surprisingly, Grimes won the Tony Award for Best Featured Actress in a Musical the following year when those awards were handed out at the annual ceremony. She went on to appear in the U.S. national tour of the show, along with Presnell with many of the other original cast members intact.

Next, thanks to the success of the show, the expected chatter soon began for a film version of the show. It was MGM who stepped up this time and won the rights. With a screenplay by Helen Deutsch, Presnell reprised his stage role for the 1964 film version. And even with all the incredible reviews Grimes had received for her work in the role, Hollywood's brutal box office demands had its way once again in Tinseltown. After the usual luminaries of the day such as Doris Day and Shirley MacLaine—and even Judy Garland—were considered, it was Debbie Reynolds who won the role after mounting a bit of a campaign to get it. She turned in a fine performance. The film was a success, winning a handful of Oscar nominations (including one for Reynolds) and was profitable for MGM. But when the sound of Oscars rang through the land that season, it was *My Fair Lady* that received the Best Picture prize, and Julie Andrews took home the Best Actress statue for her performance in *Mary Poppins*.

But Reynolds and Presnell weren't finished with *Molly* just yet. The two starred in a 1989–1990 national tour of the show. The first London production didn't open until in May 2009—an indication of the slower embracing of the show internationally.

The song "I Ain't Down Yet" became a popular standard. Musicians who recorded it included Dinah Shore in 1961 and others. The tune was also adapted as a theme song for a children's television program. NASA even got into the act: The *Gemini 3* capsule was nicknamed *Molly Brown* in reference to the musical, as Commander Gus Grissom's previous space capsule sank after splashdown.

Molly Revisited

A reading of *Molly Brown*, the first of the revised versions by writer, director, and actor Dick Scanlan, took place in Denver at the Denver Center Theatre Company's Colorado New Play Summit in February 2009. The show was directed by Kathleen Marshall and revised by Scanlan "to use more elements from the real-life story" of Molly Brown. Scanlan had known and worked with Richard Morris and knew firsthand from Morris the stories and developmental process of the original productions. Other readings followed in 2010 and 2011, again with Marshall at the helm as director and choreographer. A full production opened at the Denver Center for the Performing Arts on September 12, 2014, running through October 26. The production featured Beth Malone in the titular role with Burke Moses as Johnny. The plotline differed significantly from the original production and received favorable reviews from local reviewers and a positive notice in the *New York Times*: "A New Crew Salvages Old Molly Brown." The revised Scanlan version then opened on February 8, 2020, in previews at the off-Broadway Abrons Arts Center, presented by the Transport Group and directed and choreographed once again by Kathleen

Marshall, with Beth Malone again as Molly. The production enjoyed many positive reviews and a successful, extended run.

With *Molly*, although Meredith had not achieved the success he had with *The Music Man*, he had again helped create—and been the driving force—for *Molly*'s substantial success. He had accomplished what many have tried and failed: to have not one, but two successful shows on Broadway. The bug had bitten him, for sure. And despite suffering and enduring the grueling process of bringing not one, but two shows to Broadway, he wasn't finished trying for yet a third time.

Eighteen

FROM CLAUS TO COLUMBUS

Nothing endures but change.

—Heraclitus

Early in the 1960s, for a period of slightly more than five months, Meredith Willson had two successful shows running simultaneously on Broadway: *The Music Man* and *The Unsinkable Molly Brown*. He was now part of an exclusive list of creators who had more than one show running concurrently on Broadway. *Music Man* then closed on April 15, 1961, and *Molly* closed on February 10, 1962. Accordingly, Meredith was interested in being represented on the Great White Way with another hit once again. After all, he had reinvented himself and his career into a writer of popular Broadway musicals, so why not take the plunge for a third time? So at the age of fifty-nine, Meredith tackled his next show.

However, "the only thing permanent in this world is change," to paraphrase Heraclitus, and the United States—along with Broadway—weren't sitting still. Since *The Music Man* had opened in 1957 filled with hope and optimism, the Cold War of the 1950s had continued to grow into the 1960s, along with the tensions and fears that accompanied that increase. Racial strife in the United States was often front and center in the news. And a new musical form called rock and roll was lighting up the sales charts . . . not the musical language of Broadway at the time.

It was against this backdrop that despite or (or possibly because of) the change, upheaval, and turmoil of U.S. society, Meredith plowed ahead, well, being Meredith. Ken Kew, former mayor of Mason City, Iowa, said of him: "He was the personification of light . . . not darkness. He was a giver of joy . . . not despair."[1]

The New York theatre business was suffering because of the national mood change and stark realities of the era. Many shows produced early in the 1960s were accordingly darker in content and didn't enjoy long runs. Perhaps it was this environment that caused Meredith to gravitate to an idea that he mentioned to his longtime friend Stuart Ostrow. As previously referenced, Ostrow began his career as an apprentice of Meredith's friend and business partner in *The Music Man*, Frank Loesser. Ostrow eventually became vice president and general manager of Frank Music Corporation and Frank Productions, coproducers of Broadway shows *The Most Happy Fella*, *The Music Man*, *Greenwillow*, and *How to Succeed in Business Without Really Trying* and associated with Capitol Records, helping shepherd *The Music Man's* original cast recording to realization.

Broadway musicals are born out of any number of random occurrences, connections, and crazy ideas. They are often based on books *(South Pacific, Les Misérables)*; preexisting plays *(My Fair Lady, Hello, Dolly!)*; song catalogs *(Mama Mia, Jersey Boys)*; or films *(Grand Hotel, The Color Purple)*. So after Meredith had written a musical rooted in his Iowa roots, and then one based on a real-life person, the opportunity to create a new piece based on an existing film was new territory, not only to Meredith, but to 1960s' Broadway. Although nowadays, stage adaptations of films are much more common because the financial stakes have risen in producing a Broadway musical, producers are eager to have a known property with a built-in audience to fill a theatre.

But Meredith wasn't casting about for a film property *per se* on which to base his next musical theatre opus, but something again that captured his creative heart and soul. Perhaps Richard Rodgers's words not to take on a property or idea that he wasn't completely "possessed with" were still ringing in his ears.

Meredith and Ostrow had been bouncing several ideas back and forth, until Meredith accidentally tripped on what would become his third musical:

> When Stuart, my good friend and producer, was trying to help me dig up a story idea for a new musical, we took turns saying to each other all one afternoon, "If we could only find something a little off the ground—like

Miracle on 34th Street." I don't have to tell you what Mr. Ostrow did ultimately say. And that's how I started to write the new musical *Here's Love*,
which is based on that famous movie about a Mr. Kris Kringle.[2]

Miracle on 34th Street is a 1947 American Christmas comedy-drama film
released by Twentieth Century Fox, written and directed by George Seaton
and based on a story by Valentine Davies. It stars Maureen O'Hara, John Payne,
Natalie Wood, and Edmund Gwenn. The story takes place between Thanks-
giving Day and Christmas Day in New York City and focuses on the effect
of a department store Santa Claus who claims to be the real Santa. The film
has since been remade in various versions, most notably a 1994 feature film
directed by John Hughes starring Dylan McDermott, Elizabeth Perkins, Mara
Wilson, and Sir Richard Attenborough.

Although Meredith and Ostrow agreed the idea had potential, Meredith
was hesitant at first. He wasn't convinced that the love story could be prop-
erly developed to fulfill the requirements of a musical: Would there be enough
things to sing and dance about? Most important of all, wrote Meredith, "would
the space age accept with any interest a story about a man who thinks he's Santa
Claus?" In fact, after a few months of trial and error, Meredith was "becoming
more and more doubtful about the project. I was at that familiar point where I
was ready to give up unless somebody I could trust told me not to."[3]

That somebody was his deceased mother.

> For the last time I reviewed my outline [of the show] with a view to neat-
> ening it up before putting it back in the file—way back. It had, for some
> reason I have long since forgotten, touched here and there upon the Pro-
> logue to *Romeo and Juliet*. Wishing to quote the Bard correctly at least,
> I bethought myself of my parents' small red and gold set of Shakespeare
> which rested behind the leaded glass doors of the bookcase back home
> through most of my childhood, that is, until my mother left for a better
> world in September of 1930.[4]

The books were in his home in California, and as Meredith took down the
proper volume to do his research, he realized he had never had the occasion
to open it before. Inside the cover, he read in his mother's handwriting: "Rose

Reiniger Willson, Mason City, Iowa, Nov. 7, 1899." On the first page was pinned a newspaper clipping that had been undisturbed for so long that it had left a dark rectangle imprinted where the cover had pressed against it. The article began: "I hate these up-to-date, conscientious parents who insist upon telling their children that Santa Claus is a myth. Of course, Santa Claus is a myth, but it is the most beautiful and sweetest myth that ever found a place in rhyme and story . . . it enchants . . . and it always will."[5]

So Meredith had his confirmation from "the great beyond." Rosalie herself seemed to encourage him to continue. Meredith got to work on what he called *The Wonderful Plan* and then titled *Wouldn't It Be Wonderful.*

Variety had a front-page announcement of the show's incubation on November 29, 1961. Ostrow would make his debut as solo producer of the musical. And in his first directorial assignment, Norman Jewison was hired to direct. Jewison went on to have an illustrious career as an Academy Award–nominated director of numerous feature films, including *In the Heat of the Night* (1967), *Fiddler on the Roof* (1971), and *Moonstruck* (1987). The film's original production company, Twentieth Century Fox, had first refusal on the film rights for the property should a film version be made of the new musical.

The title of the show continued to evolve during its creation to *Love, Love, Love* and finally *Here's Love.* But the title was the least of Meredith's struggles with the show as he created it. He wrestled with his first-time process of adapting and condensing the screenplay to a stage show, while finding those key moments that needed to be musicalized. And without the help of former *Music Man* creatives Morton DaCosta and Franklin Lacey, who had been so key in the fine-tuning of that show's story and structure, he at times must have felt a bit at loose ends. However, Ostrow worked closely with him as a dramaturg and producer. The enormously talented Michael Kidd was recruited to choreograph.

As part of his writing process, Meredith pulled a song out of his trunk he wrote ten years previously, titled "It's Beginning to Look Like Christmas," which he interpolated into the show as counterpoint in the song "Pine Cones and Holly Berries." "It's Beginning . . ." by itself eventually became the longest-lasting aspect of the musical, played and performed countless times around the world and heard by millions annually at Christmastime.

Casting the show brought leading acting talent to the show: Laurence Naismith, Janis Page (after a nine-year absence from Broadway), Craig Stevens, and television's Fred Gwynne (*Car 54, Where Are You?*, and eventually *The Munsters*). Oddly enough, none of the principal actors were outstanding singers (as both *Music Man* and *Molly Brown* had in some key roles). But they were certainly good enough to get the job done. Also, a young Michael Bennett was in the chorus. Bennett would go on to conceive, choreograph, and direct the groundbreaking musical *A Chorus Line*.

In its march to Broadway, the show had its world premiere at the Fisher Theatre in Detroit on July 29, 1963. The production then moved to Washington and then Philadelphia for additional reworkings before its Broadway bow. Ostrow replaced Jewison as director at Meredith's urging, as according to Ostrow, things weren't going well during rehearsals. However, Ostrow remembers some positive aspects of his work with the show:

> My fondest memory of the musical (aside from Meredith's generosity) was the encouragement I received from the gypsy chorus. Fixing the show out of town was like a trip to the dentist; so, when after another grueling session with the stars a particularly talented dancer who had watched every rehearsal told me, "It's getting better," I believed him. His name was Michael Bennett. Our smash opening in Washington, D.C. helped boost morale, and allowed the cast and crew a hot August afternoon off to attend Martin Luther King Jr.'s Freedom March and hear his inspiring "I Have a Dream" speech.[6]

Out-of-town critical reviews were mixed, but occasionally, there were some positive notices. The *Philadelphia Enquirer* announced, "Let's skip the fancy preambles and get down to the facts . . . there is a happy show at the Shubert and that 'Music Man' Meredith Willson has done it again." On the flip side, however, *Time* magazine skewered the show: "Meredith Willson has temporarily lost his *Music Man* bounce and *Here's Love* has all the festive gaiety of a lead balloon."[7]

Ready or not, the show was heading into Manhattan.

Here's Love opened on Broadway on Thursday, October 3, 1963. Meredith's score had another spirited march included—the opening song "The Big

Clown Balloons," masterfully choreographed by Kidd—plus soaring Willson ballads and upbeat character songs. The reviews were mixed overall, yet with some positive tidbits . . . enough for the requisite "pull quotes" for advertisements and signs outside the Shubert Theatre. For example, the *New York Times* described the show as "well-engineered" and "efficient" but lacked the magic that lifted *The Music Man* into the stratosphere.[8]

A little more than a month after the show opened, history was altered when President John F. Kennedy was assassinated. The loss hit Meredith particularly hard because he had met with President Kennedy at the White House (accompanied by Rini) when the president presented him with the Big Brother Award. In 1962, the president also had recruited Meredith to write the official theme song for his youth fitness program. The march Meredith wrote, titled "Chicken Fat" was a stirring call to action for children and their families to exercise. The tragedy of the assassination cast a pall particularly over performances early in the run of *Here's Love.*

The show went on to have a decent run of 334 performances—a "soft hit" that was "profitable" according to Ostrow.[9] A cast album was recorded on Columbia Records, preserving the score and performances. Given that some shows close on opening night or after a few dozen performances at a great financial loss, that Meredith's third outing on Broadway yielded that many performances is nothing of which to be ashamed. Still, since *Here's Love* was inevitably compared to the success of his first two efforts, and critical reaction is so mixed, it felt like a flop to some. And that in that same season, the show was greatly overshadowed by two very big hits: *Hello, Dolly!* and *Funny Girl.* Therefore, *Here's Love* unfortunately boils down to not much more than a footnote in Broadway musical history.

Ostrow went on to produce other shows that enjoyed much success, among them *The Apple Tree*, *1776*, *Pippin*, and *Madame Butterfly*. He eventually transitioned to academe becoming Distinguished University Professor at the University of Houston.

Here's Love had a revival of sorts when Connecticut's Goodspeed Opera House produced it years later after its Broadway incarnation. The show then experienced yet another title change, which it carries to this day, *Miracle on 34th Street—The Musical*, and is licensed to stock and amateur theatres by Music Theatre International. So perhaps Meredith's discovery about his mama's appreciation of Santa Claus and seeming posthumous endorsement of the project were useful after all because the show lives on and is performed to this day.

Columbus Sets Sail

Even with the only modest success of *Here's Love*, Meredith continued to receive offers and connections to write yet another musical. It was *Los Angeles Times* writer Ed Ainsworth who, after a trip to Spain, envisioned a musical about the origin of the guitar—which has its roots planted in the year 1491. But after additional brainstorming, Meredith and Ed realized what was happening in Spain in 1491, the year prior to Christopher Columbus setting sail for the New World, would be infinitely riper for dramatization. Meredith and Rini became enamored with the concept. But unfortunately, tragedy was just around the corner for them.

During the fall of 1966, Meredith announced in his capacity as National Honorary Chairman of Christmas Seals during its annual kick-off program in Iowa that his beloved wife was ill with cancer. Her demise was quick; Ralina Zarova Willson died on December 6, 1966, at the age of fifty-four. Of course, Meredith was devastated.

Flowers, telegrams, cards, and notes of sympathy (including one from his first wife) poured in from around the world to Meredith during his period of grief. Rini was laid to rest in Mason City at the Elmwood-St. Joseph Cemetery.

Meredith soon threw himself back into his work, helping him cope with the loss of his greatest companion, supporter, musical sounding board, and performing partner. That work was chiefly tackling the musical that was now officially called *1491*. Prior to Rini's death, he had conducted extensive research on the life of Columbus, but due to overall incomplete and sometimes sketchy details, he chose to use a certain amount of creative license to tell the story, based on certain facts about this historic figure. The project soon garnered the attention of Edwin Lester, artistic director of the Los Angeles Civic Light Opera (LACLO), and a plan soon developed for LACLO to produce the work, then transfer it to San Francisco prior to it heading to Broadway.

During the musical's five-year birthing process, Meredith reached out—almost two years after Rini's death—to his and Rini's former secretary, Rosemary Sullivan, who was still single. Meredith invited Rosemary to dinner, and eventually a relationship developed. There's more on their history together in the Epilogue—directly from Rosemary herself. Rosemary and Meredith were married on Valentine's Day in 1968.

Rosemary was now a sounding board to Meredith with his latest musical project, *1491*. But it was a rocky road the entire voyage. Lester and Meredith clashed at every turn it seemed, due to differences of opinion in the structure and overall creative direction for the show. And although there was substantial talent not only in the lead roles (John Cullum as Columbus and Chita Rivera as his fictional mistress) along with *Molly Brown* librettist Richard Morris, whom Meredith recruited to cowrite the book when Ainsworth died suddenly, plus legendary set designer Oliver Smith (*My Fair Lady*)—these talents, along with Meredith's hard work, could not win the critics over when the show opened on September 2, 1969. The Los Angeles premiere was well-attended by curious, hopeful theatregoers who wanted to see "Meredith Music Man's" newest work. His score received praise from a few critics, but the show was savaged by all others. The *Los Angeles Herald-Examiner* called the show "desperately sincere, desperately self-important, and desperately inept."[10] Despite poor notices in Los Angeles, the show transferred to San Francisco as planned. The *San Francisco Chronicle* stated, "It is a reasonably old-fashioned musical, written by Meredith Willson with an assist from Richard Morris who directed it . . . but however grandly mounted, life, wit and the delight of theatrical surprise are not to be found in *1491*."[11]

The musical *1491* never made it past San Francisco to Broadway, closing on December 13, 1969. What turned out to be Meredith's final musical voyage was clearly his least successful. A disappointing theatrical end, but even at the age of sixty-seven, the "Unsinkable Music Man" still had a few tricks up his sleeve.

Nineteen

STILL MARCHING FORWARD

I'm not easily discouraged.

—Meredith Willson

After the disappointment of his final stage musical effort, *1491* in 1969, Meredith continued to stay busy and was in continual demand for numerous events. Now at the age of sixty-seven, he was concertizing in concert halls, colleges, and universities in a one-man show he created, telling show business stories, singing and playing the piano as he also told stories of how *The Music Man* came to be. As part of a state, local, and national marketing campaign launched in 1970 by then Iowa Governor Robert Ray, Meredith was asked to create a theme song. The campaign, and what Meredith aptly titled his song, was branded "Iowa: A Place to Grow." Meredith wrote other works into his seventies and eighties, including *A Suite for Flute* and a three-movement sacred work titled *Mass of the Bells*, in memory of his sister, Dixie, who died in 1974. In 1979, he was asked to conduct a tribute band to John Philip Sousa. As always, Rosemary accompanied him on the trip to Detroit, where the tribute was held. Sousa's grandson, John Philip Sousa III, was in the audience to witness Meredith conduct "Seventy-Six Trombones" played by the tribute band. A true full-circle moment for Meredith.

He continued as an active member and deacon of Westwood Hills Congregational Church in Los Angeles, where a stained-glass "Music Man Window" still glows to this day above his accustomed pew.

Other events of note in this next era for Meredith included leading a band of twenty-seven hundred players in Minneapolis in 1981 who had assembled to launch the city's arts week. This landed him a spot for a time in the *Guinness Book of World Records* as having led the largest marching band ever. Then, in 1982 he was invited to the Rose Bowl when the University of Iowa played the University of Washington in the celebrated football game that year. Meredith led the combined bands in the "Iowa Fight Song." This was, unfortunately, one of Meredith's last big public performances before his health started to decline. By 1983, Rosemary Willson remembered how she and others noticed the early signs of possible Alzheimer's disease:

> He was becoming more than just forgetful, because clearly his short-term memory was noticeably weak. On a visit to Mason City, as usual he stopped by the offices of the *Globe-Gazette* newspaper to visit with the editor, who introduced him to one of their reporters. After visiting with the two of them, the reporter had to excuse himself for a few minutes. When the reporter came back into the room, Meredith introduced himself to the reporter again.[1]

Meredith's health seemed to decline more and more in the months ahead. On June 8, 1984, he became ill with an intestinal obstruction and was admitted to St. John's Hospital in Santa Monica, California, not far from his and Rosemary's home in the Mandeville Canyon section of Brentwood. Rosemary describes his time in the hospital: "We thought we'd be home in a few days because they were clearing [his illness] up, but when he took a turn for the worse, his heart just gave way on him. I was with him, and I must say, he went peacefully. It was very unexpected, but he did go peacefully. He just went to sleep."[2]

Meredith passed away on June 15, 1984, at the age of eighty-two at St. John's Hospital. The Associated Press carried the story of Meredith's passing, and it echoed throughout the world. Rosemary was inundated with notes of condolence from all over, including words from Robert Preston, Debbie Reynolds, University of Iowa President James Freedman, and numerous others.[3]

Home to Mason City

Meredith could have been buried at any number of Hollywood cemeteries among many of his famous peers, but instead, not surprisingly, was laid to rest at the Elmwood-St. Joseph Municipal Cemetery in Mason City. The town's favorite son had come home to stay.

A service was held first in Los Angeles, followed by one in Mason City. The memorial service in Mason City was a fitting tribute to "America's Music Man." Rosemary described it:

> There were some wonderful surprises to me during his service. The funeral home and some others in Mason City arranged to have a barbershop quartet singing in front of Meredith's childhood home during the hearse's procession to the cemetery. They also drove us by the footbridge that was named after him. They took us to all the spots important to him where he would want to make his last visit. For them to do that was very thoughtful. I, of course, had handled all the other details of his service. But the driver of my car cautioned me as we started this tour of sentimental places that it might get to me. And it did.[4]

Many dignitaries eulogized Meredith during his service. At a reception in the basement of the Congregational Church where the service was held, Gil Lettow, band director at Mason City High School, told of when Meredith came to his band's rehearsal unexpectedly. Lettow was naturally pleasantly surprised to see the great Meredith Willson in his rehearsal room and introduced him to his students as "Mr. Willson," who promptly and politely corrected Lettow saying, "Call me Meredith," then proceeded to ask what the band was working on and encouraged them all.

Five years before *The Music Man* made its debut on Broadway, Meredith—in an interview with legendary broadcaster Edward R. Murrow—was asked by Murrow how he would like to be remembered. Meredith responded by paying tribute to a departed friend, a choral director named Max Terr, who had anonymously and humbly touched many lives. He said that Terr had taught him that "fame and fortune are fleeting, but kindness is everlasting." He went on to say:

I guess I believe pretty firmly that you don't have to be a Beethoven or a Rembrandt, or even a father, to leave a heritage to the mortal world. This is not a creed exactly . . . nor is it a complete personal objective . . . or is it? Anyhow, I think if I leave behind me any part of the kind of things that keep Max Terr alive in the hearts of his fellows, I will have justified my brief hour of strutting and fretting upon the stage.[5]

The Band Marches On

Although Meredith was now gone, his legacy lived—and lives—on. In addition to numerous productions of *The Music Man*, *The Unsinkable Molly Brown*, and *Miracle on 34th Street—The Musical*, let alone the perennial and countless airings of many versions of his song "It's Beginning to Look Like Christmas," the honors and awards have kept coming. Notably, President Ronald Reagan awarded Meredith the Presidential Medal of Freedom, the highest civilian award given, posthumously in 1987. On September 21, 1999, the U.S. Postal Service honored Meredith by issuing a postage stamp bearing his image.

In 2002, after a ten-year feasibility study, The Music Man Square museum and foundation was unveiled in Mason City. Adjoining Meredith's boyhood home, which has been restored and is open for daily tours, the work of countless people shaped this tribute to Meredith. Rosemary Willson matched dollar-for-dollar each contribution to the project, which is a magnificent complex attracting visitors from around the world. But the facility doesn't only perpetuate and pay tribute to Meredith's career and legacy; it also serves as a hub and venue for cultural events, music education, music lessons, lectures, and more. The building includes a recording studio, meeting rooms, a life-sized reproduction of the main street from *The Music Man* film, Mrs. Paroo's Gift Shop, and more. The public spaces around the facility include markers and monuments (including a life-sized statue of Meredith himself) that commemorate Meredith's career and Mason City's history.

The Julliard School of Music in New York City, his alma mater, named its new—and only—residence hall for Meredith in 2005. The Rosemary and Meredith Willson Theatre also is a part of the Julliard campus, due to a generous gift from Rosemary.

The Music Man Square, Mason City, Iowa.
COURTESY OF THE MUSIC MAN SQUARE.

The Meredith Willson Digital Collection was established at the Great American Songbook Foundation in Carmel, Indiana. Founded in 2007 by singer, pianist, producer, and music revivalist Michael Feinstein, the Great American Songbook Foundation is dedicated to preserving influential American popular songs and jazz standards from early twentieth century. It is also home to Meredith's extensive collection of papers—where much research for this book took place. The Songbook Foundation is the virtual website home of *The Meredith Willson Digital Collection*. The Digital Collection's website showcases selections from Meredith's personal archives, containing photos and musical scores dating to the 1920s; scripts from radio shows he hosted; character sketches and early drafts for *The Music Man*; personal scrapbook pages; and much more. And in 2020, the Songbook Foundation awarded Meredith its highest honor when it inducted him into their Hall of Fame.

The Music Man Foundation was founded by Rosemary in 1998 as the Meredith and Rosemary Willson Charitable Foundation and substantially increased the foundation's endowment upon her death in 2010. With a mission to support programs that use music to improve children's lives, the foundation currently focuses its investments in two initiative areas: core-curriculum music education and music therapy.

In a foreword to the libretto for *The Music Man*, Meredith gently tells all directors and performers of his show, "*The Music Man* was intended to be a Valentine and not a caricature." He was precise in his insistence that *The Music Man* be viewed as an homage to the Midwestern experience, circa 1912, that was his experience growing up. He added, "The humor of this piece depends upon its technical faithfulness to the real small-town Iowans of 1912 who certainly did not think they were funny at all."[6] So although Meredith's musical comedy contains plenty of laughs, the magical truths and serious message about the transforming power of music it imparts are alive and well in the legacy of the show and its creator. Meredith was also quoted as saying, "In my life, I went far from Mason City, but Mason City was never far from me."[7] Meredith was serious about his love and pride of and in Mason City, and Mason City was and is serious about its love of and in Meredith Willson. And millions of people are the beneficiaries of that legacy and love to this day.

EPILOGUE

The Miracle Marches On

In the 1990s, after having interviewed Rosemary Willson, widow of Meredith, by phone a year previous for a radio special I produced focusing on Meredith, I had my first in-person visit with her in her (and Meredith's) home in Los Angeles. It was in this home where Meredith wrote *The Music Man*, and the walls seemed to reverberate with its energy. Or at least the pictures and memorabilia hung on those walls and placed around the house did so, sharing the enduring legacy of his show.

As noted previously, Rini died from cancer in 1966, an obvious blow to Meredith. But life went on for Meredith in the late 1960s, and that included a serendipitous connection of the hearts, as he and Rosemary Sullivan were married on Valentine's Day in 1968. Rosemary described her and Meredith's connection to me:

> I first met him in 1941. I was living in Detroit at the time, and I used to listen to a radio program named *Maxwell House Show Boat*. The theme song for that show was "You and I," which was written by Meredith. During the summer, there was another radio show called *The Ford Sunday Evening Hour*. It had guest conductors, and Meredith was one of those conductors. So I went down after the show was over to get his autograph. That's how we first met. Then, when a girlfriend and I came to California, we arrived to see the last show of the season for *Maxwell House Show Boat*, and he arranged for us to get tickets. Then, I moved to California in 1944 to take a job with a film studio, I would go to his concert appearances, and I got to know Rini very well also. Then, when *Music Man* opened in New York in December of '57, the secretary they had decided on wanted to stay in New

York instead of going back to Los Angeles with them. And Rini said, "Why don't you give that girl a call who comes around all the time. I'm sure she's a secretary!" And that girl was Rosemary Sullivan.[1]

Rosemary worked for Meredith and Rini from 1958 to 1964. She then returned to studio work because, according to her, she did not want to lose her connections in the film industry and had received an attractive offer to return to a studio. But a great friendship had clearly developed among her, Meredith, and Rini in the years she worked for them. Then, a year after Rini had passed away, Rosemary received a call from Meredith to see if she would like to go out to dinner. According to Rosemary, "The rest was history."[2] The two eventually became engaged and married.

When I was on the phone with Rosemary, in the pre-GPS era, she gave me directions to her home, "As Meredith would always say, if the wheels on your car aren't getting ready to turn into our driveway right after you cross the small bridge, you're going to miss us!"[3] So I carefully followed Meredith's directions to reach their home and arrived, thanks to his unique and helpfully accurate description.

That sunny day in Los Angeles when I parked at the beautiful Willson home and knocked on the door, Rosemary herself answered the door and ushered me in. We sat in the den, and I was immediately captivated with a beautiful miniature version of River City on a table, a gift, she said, to Meredith from one of the uber fans of the show. There were pictures on the walls of Meredith with President John F. Kennedy, when he was awarded the Big Brother Award in recognition of his founding, extensive work, and contributions to the Los Angeles chapter of that organization. Two interlocking pianos were also in the room, both of which Meredith used at various times on which he wrote *The Music Man*. She graciously allowed me to tickle those legendary ivories, and the goose bumps I experienced were real.

The framed magazine cover/article that grabbed me the most when Rosemary told me the backstory was a *Life* magazine fold-out page that showed a parade of seventy-six actual trombones in a parade. No, it was not a still from the Warner Brothers film, but something that could only be engineered and staged by "Uncle Walt" himself.

Walt Disney had seen *The Music Man* on Broadway and was quite taken with it. He knew Meredith before he had written the show, but now his bond and respect and appreciation for Meredith's talents only grew. So, he invited Meredith and Rini to his personal dining room at Disneyland, which overlooked Main Street, USA, in the park. After a delicious meal, Walt asked Meredith to stand, and Walt brought in a tailor-made drum major's coat for Meredith to slip into. Meredith happily obliged and thought it was a fabulous gift from Walt Disney. But that was only the beginning. Walt whirled Meredith around and took him to the veranda across the room and opened the doors. He gestured for Meredith to step out onto the veranda, and there, Meredith—with Rini by his side—saw full marching band, complete with seventy-six trombones, lined up and ready to march and play! Walt then gave Meredith a conducting baton and whistle and asked him if he would do them all the pleasure of leading this band in "Seventy-Six Trombones." Meredith happily obliged, and of course, Walt had a world-class photographer take a panoramic picture of the event, which landed in the center as a fold-out picture in *Life* magazine.

The magic was real . . . and this *Music Man* band with its transforming power of music and belief was being seen from Broadway to Disney to China. And it was just beginning.

On February 10, 2022, *The Music Man* again opened on Broadway in a sparkling and triumphant new revival. This was its first Broadway revival since the Susan Stroman production of 2000. Starring Tony-winning veterans Hugh Jackman in the title role with Sutton Foster as Marian, the cast also featured Tony winners Shuler Hensley (Marcellus), Jefferson Mays (Mayor Shinn), and Jayne Houdyshell (Eulalie Mackeknie Shinn). Directed by seasoned Broadway pro Jerry Zaks, the show's choreographer was Warren Carlyle. The production was extremely well-received, and it was instantly the hottest ticket on Broadway, proving once again that Meredith's show still had legs . . . sixty-five years after its original production.

I had the pleasure and honor of attending the opening night of this new production and can write that the entire evening was pure joy. The performances were stellar, and the production was flawless. Not that there still weren't some critical pans of the new production, which is to be expected. However, most of the reviews ranged from positive to ecstatic.

The Music Man *2022 Broadway revival marquee.*
MARK CABANISS PERSONAL COLLECTION.

Till There Was Who?

Meredith Willson's legacy has been contemplated by a few biographers in far more depth than I will attempt to cover here. Meredith doesn't fit into the mold of any of his Broadway writing contemporaries because, in a sense, he had none. Since *The Music Man* opened on Broadway somewhat late in his life (he was fifty-five years old), others who had written and had their first show premiered during that era were much younger than Meredith. His career pre–*Music Man* was busy and successful overall, but eclectic, often making it hard to categorize him easily. His second Broadway outing, *The Unsinkable Molly Brown*, was a respectable hit; his third Broadway show, *Here's Love*, a solid disappointment. His final full-length show was a full-fledged flop. So with *The Music Man*, he started at the top and went progressively downhill.

But so what?

The streets of Broadway are littered with composers, lyricists, and librettists who would love nothing more than to have a single hit as powerful and lasting as *The Music Man* on their résumé (and in their bank account). But more often than not, that type of success is elusive and downright impossible. That Meredith had the courage and confidence to try again . . . and again . . . and again . . . after his wild success with *The Music Man*—when financially he didn't need to do so—is admirable, in my opinion. And his philanthropic efforts while he was alive, and now long after his death through his estate, are nothing short of incredible.

The Show That Keeps on Giving

The Music Man Foundation was founded by Rosemary Willson in 1998 as the Meredith and Rosemary Willson Charitable Foundation and substantially increased the foundation's endowment upon her death in 2010. With a mission to support programs that use music to improve children's lives, the foundation currently focuses its investments in two initiative areas: core-curriculum music education and music therapy.

Located in Mason City, Iowa, The Music Man Square is a museum filled with precious memorabilia and artifacts from the personal collection of Meredith Willson and others, revolving around Willson's life and career. Stroll down a full-scale reproduction of Main Street from the set of the Warner film version of *Meredith Willson's The Music Man*, shop in Mrs. Paroo's Gift Shop, and more.

The mission of The Music Man Square is:

- To promote, preserve, and showcase the legacy of Meredith Willson.
- To promote music, music education, and to serve as a center for music events in the community.

In addition to The Music Man Square, The Mason City Foundation exists to cultivate and support efforts to enrich the cultural environment of the community. The foundation also restored Meredith's boyhood home, which is open to the public for tours.

The Meredith Willson Digital Collection is a partnership of the Great American Songbook Foundation and HistoryIT. The website showcases a selection from the archives of Meredith Willson. The collection contains photos and musical scores dating to the 1920s; scripts from radio shows he hosted;

character sketches and early drafts for *Meredith Willson's The Music Man*; personal scrapbook pages; correspondence with such famous figures as former first lady Mamie Eisenhower, a fellow Iowa native who became a close friend; Vietnam-era letters exchanged with a nephew who later died in combat; and more.

The Great American Songbook Foundation is dedicated to preserving influential American popular songs and jazz standards from the early twentieth century. The foundation's headquarters houses a collection of compositions, recordings, scrapbooks, correspondence, and photographs from the archives of performers and composers whose work is included in the American Songbook.

To learn more about The Music Man Foundation, The Music Man Square, and The Meredith Willson Digital Collection; to peruse a gallery of pictures, audio and video clips of Meredith; and more, visit the official Meredith Willson website, www.meredithwillson.com. And to hear an exclusive, rare radio interview with Rosemary Willson conducted by me, visit www.meredithwillson.com /interview.

Meanwhile, legendary and leading music theatre licensing firm Music Theatre International (MTI) keeps licensing all of Meredith's shows year after year, decade after decade to amateur, stock, and regional theatres around the world, helping keep the legacy of "America's Music Man" and his shows alive and well.

And it all started on a simple, unassuming street in Mason City, Iowa, on May 18, 1902, when Meredith Willson was born. Little "Glory" did his parents (and Mason City) proud. And he left a legacy that reaches far beyond Broadway with no end in sight.

NOTES

Prologue

1. Personal conversation with Cy Feuer.

Chapter One

1. Meredith Willson, *And There I Stood with My Piccolo* (Minneapolis: University of Minnesota Press, 2009).

2. Ibid.

3. Ibid.

4. Ibid.

5. Personal conversation with Rosemary Willson.

6. Michael Kantor and Laurence Maslon, *Broadway: The American Musical* (Lanham, MD: Applause Books, 2004).

7. Willson, *And There I Stood with My Piccolo.*

8. Meredith Willson, "Rock Island" from *The Music Man* (Meredith Willson Music and Frank Music Corp., 1957).

9. Ibid.

10. Ibid.

11. Richard Colwell, Michael Hewitt, and Mark Fonder, *The Teaching of Instrumental Music*, 5th ed. (New York: Routledge, 2017).

Chapter Two

1. Bill Oates, *Meredith Willson: America's Music Man* (Bloomington, IN: Bill Oates, 2005).

2. Meredith Willson, *But He Doesn't Know the Territory* (New York: G. P. Putnam's Sons, 1959).

3. Oates, *America's Music Man*.

4. Meredith Willson, "My White Knight" from *The Music Man* (Meredith Willson Music and Frank Music Corp., 1957).

5. Willson, *But He Doesn't Know the Territory*.

6. Ibid.

7. Willson, *And There I Stood with My Piccolo*.

8. Willson, *But He Doesn't Know the Territory*.

9. Dixie Willson, *Honey Bear* (Los Angeles: Silver Starlight Books, 2014).

10. Oates, *America's Music Man*.

11. Ibid.

12. Ibid.

13. John C. Skipper, *Meredith Willson: The Unsinkable Music Man* (Mason City, IA: Savas Publishing Company).

Chapter Three

1. Willson, *And There I Stood with My Piccolo*.

2. Personal conversation with Rosemary Willson.

3. Willson, *And There I Stood with My Piccolo*.

4. Ibid.

5. Personal conversation with Rosemary Willson.

6. Oates, *America's Music Man*.

7. Meredith Willson, "Seventy-Six Trombones" from *The Music Man* (Meredith Willson Music and Frank Music Corp., 1957).

8. Oates, *America's Music Man*.

Chapter Four

1. Skipper, *The Unsinkable Music Man*.
2. Ibid.
3. Ibid.
4. Oates, *America's Music Man*.
5. Ibid.
6. Ibid.
7. Meredith Willson, *Eggs I Have Laid* (New York: Henry Holt and Company, 1955).
8. Skipper, *The Unsinkable Music Man*.
9. Willson, *And There I Stood with My Piccolo*.

Chapter Five

1. Willson, *Eggs I Have Laid*.
2. Personal conversation with Rosemary Willson.
3. Willson, *Eggs I Have Laid*.
4. Miles Kreuger, ed. *The Movie Musical from Vitaphone to 42nd Street as Reported in a Great Fan Magazine* (Mineola, NY: Dover Publications, 1974).
5. Mordaunt Hall, "The Screen," *New York Times*, February 3, 1930.
6. Willson, *Eggs I Have Laid*.
7. Personal conversation with Rosemary Willson.
8. Oates, *America's Music Man*.
9. Ibid.
10. Personal conversation with Rosemary Willson.
11. Willson, *Eggs I Have Laid*.
12. Ibid.
13. Ibid.
14. Ibid.

Chapter Six

1. Meredith Willson, and Rini Willson, *And Then I Wrote* The Music Man (Los Angeles: Capitol Records, 1959).

2. Ibid.

3. Willson, *And There I Stood with My Piccolo*.

4. Ibid.

5. Ibid.

6. Ibid.

7. Bosley Crowther, "'The Little Foxes' Full of Evil, Reaches the Screen," *New York Times*, August 22, 1941.

8. Willson, *And There I Stood with My Piccolo*.

9. Ibid.

10. "Never Feel Too Weary to Pray," Words © 1941 Meredith Willson Music. All Rights Reserved. Used by Permission.

11. Willson, *And There I Stood with My Piccolo*.

12. Ibid.

Chapter Seven

1. Willson, *But He Doesn't Know the Territory*.

2. Ibid.

3. Ibid.

4. Willson, *Eggs I Have Laid*.

5. Personal conversation with Virginia Waring.

6. Willson, *And There I Stood with My Piccolo*.

7. Willson, *But He Doesn't Know the Territory*.

8. Ibid.

9. Ibid.

Chapter Eight

1. Willson, *But He Doesn't Know the Territory*.

2. Ibid.

3. Ibid.

4. Ibid.

5. Ibid.

6. Ibid.

7. Ibid.

8. Ibid.

9. Ibid.

10. "My White Knight," Words © 1957 Meredith Willson Music and Frank Music Corporation. All Rights Reserved.

11. Willson, *But He Doesn't Know the Territory*.

12. Ibid.

13. Ibid.

14. Ibid.

15. Personal conversation with Cy Feuer.

16. Willson, *But He Doesn't Know the Territory*.

17. Ibid.

18. Ibid.

19. Ibid.

20. Ibid.

21. Ibid.

Chapter Nine

1. Personal conversation with Cy Feuer.

2. Willson, *But He Doesn't Know the Territory*.

3. Ibid.

4. Ibid.

5. Ibid

6. Ibid.

7. Ibid.

8. Ibid.

9. Ibid.

10. Ibid.

11. Personal conversation with Cy Feuer.

12. Willson, *But He Doesn't Know the Territory*.

13. Ibid.

14. Ibid.

15. Ibid.

16. Ibid.

17. Ibid.

18. Ibid.

19. Ibid.

20. Ibid.

21. Ibid.

22. Ibid.

23. Ibid.

24. Ibid.

25. Ibid.

26. Ibid.

27. Ibid.

28. Personal conversation with Cy Feuer.

Chapter Ten

1. Willson, *But He Doesn't Know the Territory*.

2. Ibid.

3. Ibid.

4. Ibid.

5. Ibid.

6. Ibid.

7. Ibid.

8. Ibid.

9. Ibid.

10. Ibid.

11. Richard Armstrong, *The Music Man*, *Time*, July 21, 1958.

12. Willson, *But He Doesn't Know the Territory*.

13. Ibid.

14. Meredith Willson, "Till There Was You" from *The Music Man* (Meredith Willson Music and Frank Music Corp., 1957).

Chapter Eleven

1. Willson, *But He Doesn't Know the Territory*.
2. Ibid.
3. Ibid.
4. Ibid.
5. Ibid.
6. Ibid.
7. Ibid.
8. Ibid.
9. Ibid.
10. Ibid.
11. Ibid.
12. Ibid.
13. Ibid.
14. Ibid.
15. Meredith Willson, "Rock Island" from *The Music Man* (Meredith Willson Music and Frank Music Corp., 1957).
16. Willson, *But He Doesn't Know the Territory*.

Chapter Twelve

1. Willson, *But He Doesn't Know the Territory*.
2. Ibid.
3. Ibid.
4. Armstrong, *The Music Man*.
5. Personal conversation with Eddie Hodges.
6. Willson, *But He Doesn't Know the Territory*.
7. Meredith Willson, "My White Knight" from *The Music Man* (Meredith Willson Music and Frank Music Corp., 1957).
8. Ibid.

9. Jo Swerling, Abe Burrows, and Frank Loesser, "I'll Know" from *Guys and Dolls* (Frank Music Corp., 1951).

10. Meredith Willson, "Essay," *Herald Tribune*, New York, 1957.

11. Meredith Willson, *The Music Man* (Meredith Willson Music and Frank Music Corp., 1957).

12. Meredith Willson, "Ya Got Trouble" from *The Music Man* (Meredith Willson Music and Frank Music Corp., 1957).

Chapter Thirteen

1. Willson, *But He Doesn't Know the Territory*.

2. Ibid.

3. Barbara Cook, *Then and Now—A Memoir* (New York: HarperCollins, 2016).

4. Willson, *But He Doesn't Know the Territory*.

5. Ibid.

6. Ibid.

7. Charles Champlin, *The Music Man*—and His Song, *Los Angeles Times* (March 23, 1987).

8. Willson, *But He Doesn't Know the Territory*.

9. Willson, "Ya Got Trouble" from *The Music Man* (Meredith Willson Music and Frank Music Corp., 1957).

10. Willson, *But He Doesn't Know the Territory*.

Chapter Fourteen

1. Willson, *But He Doesn't Know the Territory*.

2. Ibid.

3. Ibid.

4. Ibid.

5. Ibid.

6. Ibid.

7. Personal conversation with Rosemary Willson.

8. Stuart Ostrow, *A Producer's Broadway Journey* (Westport, CT: Praeger Publishers, 1999).

9. Willson, *But He Doesn't Know the Territory.*

10. Ibid.

11. Ibid.

12. Ibid.

13. Ibid.

14. Ibid.

15. Ibid.

16. Ibid.

17. Ibid.

18. Ibid.

19. Ibid.

20. Ibid.

21. Ibid.

22. Ibid.

23. Ibid.

Chapter Fifteen

1. Kantor and Maslon, *Broadway.*

2. Willson, *But He Doesn't Know the Territory.*

3. Ibid.

4. Ibid.

5. Ibid.

6. Ibid.

7. Cook, *Then and Now.*

8. Willson, *But He Doesn't Know the Territory.*

9. Armstrong, *The Music Man.*

10. Personal conversation with Cy Feuer.

11. Personal conversation with Rosemary Willson.

Chapter Sixteen

1. Meredith Willson to Julius Lefkowitz, letter, May 29, 1959. Great American Songbook Foundation.
2. Personal conversation with Rosemary Willson.
3. Morton DaCosta to Meredith Willson, letter June 11, 1960. Great American Songbook Foundation.
4. Personal conversation with Shirley Jones.
5. Ibid.
6. Ibid.
7. Ibid.
8. Ron Howard and Clint Howard, *The Boys: A Memoir of Hollywood and Family* (New York: William Morrow and Company, 2021).
9. Personal conversation with Shirley Jones.
10. Ibid.
11. Ibid.
12. Ibid.
13. Mason City *Globe-Gazette*, 1962 clipping. Great American Songbook Foundation.
14. Ibid.
15. Bosley Crowther, *New York Times*, August 24, 1962.
16. Personal conversation with Rosemary Willson.
17. Shirley Jones, *The Music Man* (film version), bonus feature interview.

Chapter Seventeen

1. Meredith Willson, "Broadway Meditation," *Philadelphia Inquirer*, 1960.
2. Ibid.
3. Ibid.
4. Dore Schary, *The Unsinkable Molly Brown* Broadway cast recording liner notes (Capitol Records, 1960).
5. Willson, *Broadway Meditation*.
6. Ibid.
7. Ibid.

8. Ibid.

9. David Foil, *The Unsinkable Molly Brown* Broadway cast recording liner notes (Capitol Records, 1960).

Chapter Eighteen

1. Kenneth Kew, Meredith Willson eulogy, Mason City, Iowa, 1984.

2. Meredith Willson, *Here's Love* Broadway cast recording liner notes (Capitol Records, 1962).

3. Ibid.

4. Ibid.

5. Note from Rosalie Willson, November 7, 1899.

6. Ostrow, *A Producer's Broadway Journey.*

7. Didier Deutsch, *Here's Love* Broadway cast recording CD liner notes (Capitol Records, 1992).

8. Ibid.

9. Ostrow, *A Producer's Broadway Journey.*

10. *Los Angeles Herald* clipping, 1969. Great American Songbook Foundation.

11. *San Francisco Chronicle* clipping, 1969. Great American Songbook Foundation.

Chapter Nineteen

1. Conversation with Rosemary Willson.

2. Ibid.

3. Clippings from Meredith Willson papers/archives, The Great American Songbook Foundation, Carmel, IN.

4. Conversation with Rosemary Willson.

5. Clippings from Meredith Willson papers/archives, The Great American Songbook Foundation, Carmel, IN.

6. Meredith Willson, *The Music Man* libretto (Meredith Willson Music and Frank Music Corp., 1957).

7. Conversation with Rosemary Willson.

Epilogue

1. Conversation with Rosemary Willson.
2. Ibid.
3. Ibid.

INDEX

Page references for photos are italicized.

Songs

ABOUT THE AUTHOR

Mark Cabaniss is a music publisher, writer/producer, broadcaster, and educator. He is president and CEO of Jubilate Music Group, creating printed and digital music, recordings, and videos.

As an ASCAP composer and arranger, Cabaniss's published compositions have been performed nationally and abroad and include musicals, cantatas, and instrumental works. He is a multiple recipient of ASCAP's Popular Music Award and is a Dove Award and Angel Award–winning producer. For his contributions to the music products industry, NAMM awarded him the *Believe in Music* Award. He is a member of The Recording Academy (Grammy), The Dramatists Guild, and serves on the board of advisors for "The Music Man Square," a museum and foundation in Mason City, Iowa, dedicated to furthering music education and honoring the legacy of Meredith Willson.

Cabaniss was named Outstanding Alumnus of the Year by Mars Hill University and serves on the University's Board of Trustees. He is also the founder and donor of The Helen Cole Krause Music Scholarship, awarded annually to qualifying students who choose music as a college major.

He also serves as a correspondent for *Hollywood 360*, a weekly nationally syndicated entertainment radio show based in Chicago.

His more-than-thirty-year career in music business and broadcasting has led to collaborations with television icons Bob Barker, Kathie Lee Gifford, and Andy Griffith; Academy Award–winner Shirley Jones; legendary entertainer Steve Allen; Broadway/pop songwriters Rupert Holmes and David Pomeranz; jazz pianist/composer Loonis McGlohon; composer Charles Strouse; and others.

Cabaniss also serves as an adjunct instructor of music business at Belmont University in Nashville. He holds bachelor's and master's degrees in Music Education and Communications from Mars Hill University and the University of Tennessee, Knoxville. He resides in Nashville.

www.markcabaniss.com